INVESTMENT TAX PLANNING GUIDE

2nd Edition

Seth Hammer

CCH INCORPORATED
Chicago
A WoltersKluwer Company

Editorial Staff

Production . . . . Jennifer Schencker

Index . . . . Lynn Brown

Investment Tax Planning Guide was previously published by **CCH** INCORPO-RATED as *Investments and Taxes: A Practical Guide for Financial Advisors.*

ISBN 0-8080-1189-8

©2004, **CCH** INCORPORATED
4025 W. Peterson Ave.
Chicago, IL 60646-6085
1 800 248 3248
http://tax.cchgroup.com

For Beverly and Emma

Preface

Investment Tax Planning Guide was published in its First Edition in 2002 as *Investments and Taxes: A Practical Guide for Financial Advisors.* In the spirit of the book itself, which is concisely written, the title was simplified and trimmed down.

Investment Tax Planning Guide, drawing on a multitude of well-documented research findings, provides numerous strategies for optimizing the use of tax-advantaged investments and vehicles. Most importantly, the guidance is both *specific* and *practical,* providing advisors immediate opportunities to increase their clients' after-tax returns and to better manage their exposure to financial risk.

The guide, described as "an essential book for any complete financial planning library" (1st edition review, *Journal of the American Taxation Association*), has been fully updated to reflect the *Jobs and Growth Tax Relief Reconciliation Act of 2003,* other relevant tax law changes, and new developments and research discoveries.

Whether advisers are seeking to "tweak" a portfolio or develop an all-new financial plan, *Investment Tax Planning Guide* provides advisors with practical information that can be used to assist clients in achieving their financial goals.

Seth Hammer

June 2004

About the Author

SETH HAMMER is an associate professor of accounting at Towson University in Towson, Maryland. He holds a Ph.D. from the University of Pittsburgh, an M.B.A. (specialization in taxation) from Baruch College, City University of New York, and a B.S. degree from Syracuse University. He is a C.P.A. and a C.M.A. His articles have appeared in the *Tax Advisor*, the *CPA Journal*, and the *Journal of Asset Protection* (co-author). Dr. Hammer has been a speaker at educational programs for accounting professionals and academics. Dr. Hammer has been providing financial education programs for members of the National Football League's Baltimore Ravens since 1996, the team's inaugural year in that city. He is a member of the AICPA and the Maryland Association of Certified Public Accountants.

Acknowledgments

In appreciation of Professor Jacob G. Birnberg, University of Pittsburgh, whose wisdom, integrity and humor have inspired a generation of doctoral students.

Table of Contents

Chapter 9: Retirement Funding

Chapter 1

INTRODUCTION

¶101 Overview

The purpose of this book is to provide an overview of practical tax planning strategies that can be incorporated into an overall financial and estate plan. The means of achieving it, as is commonly the case in professional practice, are presented from two distinct perspectives:

1. **Portfolio perspective.** Investors typically strive to maintain and grow a portfolio of stocks, bonds, real estate and other investments. Although the amount apportioned for each of the asset types will vary, depending largely upon total wealth, current and projected income, and a taxpayer's attitude towards risk, the concept of holding a mix of asset types commonly forms the framework for more detailed planning. Part One of this book, (Chapters 2 through 6) *"Portfolio Perspective: Practical Tax Planning Strategies for Investing with Stocks, Bonds, Real Estate, Derivatives and Annuities,"* describes how investors holding or considering holding the aforementioned asset types can apply practical tax reduction strategies to optimize their performance for each of these categories within an overall portfolio.

2. **Goal perspective.** Investors, while seeking to build a portfolio comprised of assets providing optimal opportunities for growth and risk control, also commonly seek to achieve specific goals, such as the funding of a child's education. Part Two of this book, (Chapters 7 through 10) *"Goal Perspective: Practical Tax Planning Strategies for Charitable Contributions, College Funding, Retirement Funding, and Gifts and Estates,"* describes practical tax reduction strategies that can be utilized to achieve goals in each of those areas. Emphasis, in this section, is placed largely on how to evaluate and make the most practical choice amongst the myriad vehicles available for tax deferral and/or tax exclusion in order to help the client successfully achieve a specific desired financial goal.

The term "practical" is key in the elements of tax planning strategies presented in this book. A viable tax planning strategy considers not only opportunities for tax savings, but also these other factors:

- Investment Costs and Operating Expenses,
- Market Risk,
- Investment Risk,
- Liquidity Risk,
- Legislative Risk [especially after EGTRRA '01 and JGTRRA '03], and
- Monitoring Effort.

Example 1: Sally Jane Smith is considering making an additional investment for the equities portion of her portfolio. If she is most concerned about tax minimization, she is likely to consider individual growth stocks that she would hold for an extended period of time. This choice could potentially provide her with at least three important tax-related benefits:

1. **Opportunity to control time for recognizing gains and/or losses.** Direct ownership of equities, rather than through a conduit (e.g., fund), best allows investors opportunities to time the recognition of capital gains and/ or losses. The owner of shares in a fund, alternatively, has no control over the passthroughs of gains and losses, which could come at inopportune times.

2. **Opportunity to minimize income recognized at ordinary income tax rates.** Stocks, as compared to other investments such as bonds and real estate investment trusts, provide opportunities to recognize income at reduced rates (e.g., maximum rate of 15 percent on long-term capital gains and dividends).

3. **Opportunity to maximize compounding benefits.** Growth stocks, as compared to value stocks, provide greater opportunities to maximize the benefits of compounding, by virtue of their lower distributions. This factor may be more of an issue for investors who are subject to high state and local taxes.

The purchase of individual shares of stocks may be impractical, however, because of one or any combination of the following factors:

1. **Investment costs.** If the size of the purchase is not sufficiently large, the cost of commissions may make this choice impractical as compared to other choices, such as a mutual fund.

2. **Market risk.** If the taxpayer only has stock investments, then the taxpayer may be placing herself at unnecessary risk, as compared to an investor who holds a more broadly diversified portfolio (e.g., stocks, bonds and real estate).

3. **Investment risk.** If the taxpayer does not have a diversified set of equity investments, she may be placing herself at unnecessary risk of holding a portfolio that will decline in value even as the broader equity market increases in value. She may also be subject to a tax-related investment risk, as would be the case if she incurred losses in excess of the $3,000 maximum annual allowance.

4. **Liquidity risk.** If the stock is not widely traded, there is the risk that the stock either cannot be sold or will be subject to a costly bid/ask spread.

5. **Legislative risk.** The preferred capital gains rates, for example, may not necessarily remain in effect. Prior legislation has raised, as well as decreased, the tax rate on capital gains.

6. **Monitoring effort.** If only a small group of stocks is held, the investor may need to be extra vigilant to ensure the ability to act in the event of a major corporate event that could cause the value of the stock to plummet (e.g., CEO resignation and/or lawsuit).

The challenge for the planner, therefore, is to evaluate investment opportunities in the context of these practical considerations. Certainly, the purchase of individual growth stocks may make sense for an individual who:

1. Incurs low transaction costs (e.g., on-line trading),

2. Has a diversified portfolio of equities and other investments,

3. Can easily liquidate the stock (e.g., traded on the New York Stock Exchange) or has sufficient other liquid assets,

4. Is not dependent upon the preferred capital gains rate, and

5. Is willing to make the necessary monitoring effort. If, however, one or more of these factors is not met, then the planner may need to seek out more viable alternatives. See ¶102 for discussion of how this book may be used to seek out the more viable alternatives.

¶102 Using This Book for Practical Advantage—Illustrations

Two brief illustrations of how this book may aid the adviser are shown below.

> **Example 2:** Continuation of Example 1. Taxpayer desires a more practical tax-advantaged alternative to the strategy of holding individual growth stocks.

The adviser seeking to find practical equity alternatives to individual growth stock investments could begin by reviewing relevant sections of Chapter 2, "*Stock Investments.*" These sections are most likely to include paragraphs 201 through 212, which cover individual stocks, managed funds, index funds, exchange-traded funds, and tax-managed funds. An adviser, alternatively, could take a more targeted approach, in cases, for example, where she requires information for only one particular form of investing (e.g., tax-managed funds covered in ¶212).

Relevant findings from the aforementioned sections for the adviser might include:

1. Exchange-traded funds may potentially offer the best opportunity for tax deferral, but have a short track record in most areas of investing. Some thinly traded funds may generate significant bid/ask spreads.

2. Index funds may offer the lowest-cost opportunity for acquisitions and redemptions. Only funds based on certain indexes, however, generate significant opportunities for tax deferral.

3. The *pre-tax* performance of index funds has been consistently higher than that of managed funds in some sectors, such as in large capitalization stocks, but not in others, according to *Morningstar*. Importantly, these findings do not appear to be random, and provide a meaningful benchmark in determining where to best utilize index-based investments.

4. Some managed funds are *closet-indexers,* meaning that their performance is highly correlated with some underlying index. In most cases, the net returns of these funds do not outweigh their added management costs.

5. Tax-managed funds may provide excellent tax deferral opportunities, but may also subject the investor to significant detriments including 1) higher operating costs than index funds, 2) potentially increasing exposure to built-in gains and 3) risk of sub-par pre-tax performance arising from constraints of tax-managed style.

6. Funds that have large loss carryforwards (e.g., some technology and/or aggressive growth funds) may provide even better tax benefits than tax-managed funds. The often volatile nature of these funds may make them viable, however, only for those taxpayers who are willing to assume a greater level of risk and/or already hold a very widely diversified portfolio.

Based on these and related findings the adviser might well recommend the use of one or more of these alternative vehicles. The adviser, for example, might recommend the use of exchange-traded funds for large capitalization stocks to obtain maximum tax deferral in this area. In this case, the choice potentially providing the greatest opportunity for long-term tax deferral may also be the most practical one. Exchange traded shares for large capitalization stocks are available that:

1. Are reasonably well established,

2. Can be purchased and sold with minimal transaction costs, and

3. Are subject to minimal bid/ask spreads.

In cases of equities other than large capitalization stocks, however, the adviser might recommend the following practical choices that provide significant, but not necessarily the largest, tax benefits:

1. **S&P SmallCap 600 based index fund for small capitalization stock investments.** Although exchange-traded funds are likely to provide greater opportunities for tax-deferral, such funds may not be the preferred choice for long-term investing in the small capitalization area, because they have not been in existence for a long enough period of time to provide sufficient comfort for the client. Although a *Russell 2000* based fund provides coverage of a somewhat broader market, an *S&P Small-Cap 600* based fund is chosen because:

    a. It provides sufficiently broad coverage of the small capitalization market, and

b. Typically has a lower turnover ratio, providing for better opportunities for deferral of capital gains.

2. **Managed [not "closet-indexer"] fund for international investments.** The adviser may determine that some managed international funds, despite higher management costs and higher turnover, provide the opportunity for higher after-tax returns. The adviser may, however, before finalizing the choice of a specific managed fund, evaluate it to determine whether it is a "closet-indexer." If so, the adviser may find that an index fund may be available that provides comparable pre-tax performance at lower investment cost.

Example 3: Thomas Heard is attempting to determine the best opportunities for saving to fund his children's education. Unlike the previous examples, where the investor knew she wanted to invest in equities, Mr. Heard is uncertain as to what forms of investment to use. Further, with so many opportunities available for tax-exempt or tax-deferred investing (e.g., qualified tuition programs, Coverdell Education Savings Accounts, and U.S. Savings Bonds), he is not certain as to the appropriate starting point.

The adviser searching for the most optimal funding methods for his client could begin by reviewing the paragraph headings for Chapter 8, "*College Funding.*" If the adviser is not very familiar with the relative benefits/detriments of the various vehicles for college funding, he may find it beneficial to at least skim all of the sections in order to form a meaningful basis for comparison. Alternatively, if the adviser has a good understanding of the various forms of college funding, he could limit his review by focusing on a particular section (e.g., "Coverdell Education Savings Accounts—A Second Best Option for Many, First Best for a Few").

The optimal choice(s) of tax-deferred/exempt vehicle for college funding is likely to vary significantly, depending upon an individual family's situation. While many middle-income taxpayers may find Roth IRAs and Coverdell Education Savings Accounts to provide the best opportunities for tax savings and investing flexibility, higher income taxpayers, who are precluded from benefiting from such vehicles, may find Section 529 Qualified Tuition Programs to provide the most practical choice. A review of ¶803.03, may alert the adviser, however, that qualified *prepaid tuition* programs may, in fact, be a very impractical solution for families seeking to obtain financial aid for their children. That section explains that the amount of funds contained in such a plan generally reduces a student's potential for financial aid on a *dollar-for-dollar* basis. That same section may, nonetheless, aid the adviser by explaining that the alternative form of Section 529 Qualified Tuition Programs, qualified *savings* programs, may offer a viable choice, since the assets contained in such an account are considered, for financial aid purposes, to be an asset of the parent, assuming that the account is owned by a parent of the student.

¶103 Asset Allocation—A Key to Successful Investing

A key consideration in the development of any financial portfolio should include the factor of *strategic asset allocation.* This is the allocation amongst different classes of assets, such as stocks, bonds, and real estate. Strategic allocation can be used to reduce the risk that all components of a portfolio will decline in value simultaneously. Therefore, a well-balanced portfolio should contain a variety of stock sizes (e.g., large, mid-size, and small) and styles (value and growth), as well as bonds and real estate. Advisers who are reviewing their clients' portfolios to increase diversification may benefit by reviewing sections of this book that provide practical recommendations for achieving that objective, along with practical tax planning strategies. An adviser, for example, seeking a practical way to incorporate real estate into his client's portfolio may find that real estate investment trusts (REITs) provide viable opportunities to generate increased portfolio diversification, while maintaining greater liquidity than is typically associated with more traditional forms of real estate ownership, such as limited partnerships.

The apportionment of assets between taxable and tax-deferred or tax-exempt accounts can have a significant impact, of course, on after-tax income. While the conventional approach has typically been to apportion assets subject primarily to ordinary income recognition, such as bonds, to tax-deferred accounts, and assets primarily subject to capital gains taxation, such as stocks, to taxable accounts, recent research has determined that this strategy is often not optimal. Readers, therefore, not familiar with the *Beardsley*[1] study, which examined this issue, are encouraged to review ¶904, "Unconventional Approach to Asset Apportionment for Retirement Planning May Yield Significant Benefits," before embarking upon a plan of asset apportionment.

Asset allocation also should be considered when developing a strategy to maintain maximum flexibility for future contingencies. I-bonds, for example, can allow a taxpayer to defer income recognition for up to thirty years or, alternatively, in some cases may allow for income exclusion where the proceeds are used for college tuition. If needed, however, for any reason (e.g., purchase of a vacation house and/or medical expenses) they can be cashed after being held for more than five years without penalty, even where the taxpayer is under age 59 1/2. As a practical consideration, therefore, a number of taxpayers may prefer to apportion some of their long-term assets outside of the retirement account, even though there is some potential loss of tax deferral.

Advisers should also keep in mind that development of an optimal asset allocation pattern is an ongoing process and that changes in life stages may create new opportunities for implementing practical tax planning strategies. A retired individual, who, for example, in an earlier life stage may not have been a good candidate for a fixed annuity, may find that it now offers favorable opportunities to mitigate risk while also deferring taxes.

---

[1] "Deciding Which Funds to Hold in Taxable vs. Tax-Deferred Accounts," by Samuel F. Beardsley, *www.troweprice.com/taxstrategy/decide.html.*

¶103

Chapter 2

STOCK INVESTMENTS

¶201 Stocks—A Tax-Advantaged Investment Is Made Significantly More Attractive by the Jobs and Growth Tax Relief Reconciliation Act of 2003 (JGTRRA)

Investments in stocks prior to the passage of JGTRRA provided, in general, the dual benefits of excellent long-term returns and tax-preferred status. During the period of 1926-1999, for example, large capitalization common stocks provided a compound annual return of 11.3 percent,[1] with most of the income being subject to preferred tax rates of 20 percent or less.[2] Normally, only the dividend portion of the income, typically just one to two percent per year, was subject to tax at marginal ordinary income rates.

Passage of JGTRRA makes stock investments potentially even more attractive by reducing the maximum tax rate for most long-term capital gains to 15 percent (5 percent for taxpayers in lower marginal tax brackets) and extending the same tax-advantaged rates to qualifying dividends. Additionally, dividends from preferred stocks may also qualify for these tax-advantaged rates. As a result of these reductions, investors may consider increasing the portions of their portfolios that are allocated to stocks, both common and preferred.

An additional enhancement of the new tax rates for dividends and long-term capital gains is that they also apply for purposes of the alternative minimum tax.[3] In the case of qualifying small business stock, a further benefit is that the amount of excluded gain treated as a tax preference has been reduced from 42 percent to 7 percent.[4] See ¶213 for more details.

.01 Qualifying Dividends

Reduced tax rates (i.e., 15 percent and 5 percent) apply to corporate distributions from domestic corporations and qualifying foreign corporations. Distributions from foreign corporations that are traded on an established U.S. securities market are considered qualified.[5] Additionally, non-U.S. stocks may be eligible for qualifying dividend status in certain cases where treaty requirements are met.[6]

---

[1] Assumes no transaction costs and that all cash flows are reinvested at month-end.

[2] Assuming, in most cases, that the stock was held for more than one year.

[3] Code Sec. 55(b)(3)(B) and (C) as amended by the 2003 Act.

[4] Code Sec. 57(a)(7) as amended by the 2003 Act.

[5] Code Sec. 1(h)(11(C)(ii) as amended by the 2003 Act.

[6] Code Sec. 1(h)(11)(C)(i) as amended by the 2003 Act.

A distribution is generally considered to be a dividend to the extent that it is paid out of earnings and profits.[7] There is no requirement, however, as had been recommended in the President's original tax cut proposal, that dividends be derived from taxed corporate earnings.[8]

Distributions from mutual funds will qualify for the reduced rates, assuming that the dividends received from the payors by the mutual fund company would qualify for such rates. Certain other distributions, including some labeled as "dividends," such as those paid by credit unions and mutual insurance companies do not qualify for reduced rates.

> **TAX PLANNING:** Owners of closely-held corporations may find it beneficial to decrease officer salary payments and increase dividend payments in cases where the salary distribution would be subject to high marginal tax rates, including Medicare taxes (imposed on the individual as both owner and employee) and state unemployment taxes. While for many taxpayers the optimal goal for income subject to corporate tax rates would be exactly $50,000, the maximum level of income subject to tax at the 15-percent marginal tax rate, such fine-tuning may not be possible because of "reasonable salary" requirements.

> **PRACTICE POINTER:** While dividend paying stocks have become more attractive following the reduction in tax rates enacted by JGTRRA, investors may wonder, strictly from a financial perspective, whether high dividend paying stocks perform better, worse, or comparably to lower or non-dividend paying stocks. Research conducted by Robert D. Arnott and Clifford S. Asness suggests, based on historical data, that future earnings growth will be faster for those companies that have higher payout ratios than for those companies that have lower payout ratios.[9] These findings contradict the views of those individuals who believe that reinvestment, rather than distributions of earnings, will lead to faster growth. An open question is whether this model will apply in a new environment where companies whom, otherwise, would not be predisposed to pay high dividends, will increase them simply to meet perceived market demands for higher payouts.

.02 Ineligible Dividends

The following dividend distributions do not qualify for the reduced tax rate:

1. From corporations exempt from income tax under Section 501,[10]

2. Amounts allowed as deductions for dividends paid on deposits (e.g., deposits of mutual savings banks),[11]

---

[7] Code Sec. 316.

[8] For further discussion see *Jobs and Growth Tax Relief Reconciliation Act of 2003: Law, Explanation and Analysis*, CCH, Chicago, 2003.

[9] "Surprise! Higher Dividends=Higher Earnings Growth," by Robert D. Arnott and Clifford S. As-

ness, *Financial Analysts Journal*, January/February 2003, Vol. 59 (1), pp. 70-87.

[10] Code Sec. 1(h)(11)(B)(ii) as added by the 2003 Act.

[11] *Ibid.*

3. From real estate investment trusts, with limited exceptions,[12]

4. Stock held for less than 60 days during the 120-day period surrounding the ex-dividend date,[13]

5. Substitute payments made in lieu of a dividend, for loaned stock in a short sale, and

6. certain types of preferred stock [see below].

TAX PLANNING: Investors may achieve a modest tax benefit by investing in funds that hold stocks and bonds together (e.g., a balanced fund), rather than in separate funds. Expenses in such funds are first offset against interest income and short-term capital gains, neither subject to preferred tax rates, before being offset against qualifying dividends and long-term capital gains, both of which qualify for preferred rates.

.03 Preferred Stock Dividends

Passage of JGTRRA may make investments in preferred stock a more attractive alternative to bonds because the dividends, unlike interest payments of bonds, are subject to the tax-advantaged rates. Investors who are considering preferred stocks, because of their tax-advantaged rates, should be sure that the instrument actually qualifies for reduced tax-rate status.

PRACTICE POINTER: Many instruments marketed as "preferred stock" are actually trusts that pay interest and, accordingly, do not qualify for the reduced tax rates. Another concern is that many preferred stocks are callable. U.S. Bankcorp's B shares, for example, carry a 7.75-percent issue, but may be called as of May 2006, limiting the investor's ability to achieve a long-term lock-in of rates.[14] Alternatively, should market rates increase and/or a bond's credit worthiness decline, the investor does not have a fixed redemption date, at which point the instrument could otherwise be redeemed for its face value.

.04 Dividends and the Investment Income Limitation

Qualifying dividend income is not considered to be investment income, for purposes of determining the investment interest limitation, unless the taxpayer elects to treat it as such and, thereby, forfeit the benefit of the reduced tax rate.[15] Interest expense that is currently disallowed because of investment income limitations may, however, still be carried forward indefinitely to future periods.

Despite this statutory limitation many taxpayers, especially those of higher income levels, will be able to benefit from the differential between the preferred

---

[12] Dividends generally do not qualify because the distributions are deductible by the REIT. In cases, however, where earnings were subject to the corporate income tax, they may qualify for the reduced rate.

[13] Code Sec. 1(h)(11)(B)(iii), as added by the 2003 Act.

[14] This issue, including the U.S. Bankcorp example, is discussed in more detail in "Wall Street Pushes Preferred Stock; Tax Cuts Spur Interest in Dividend Rich Shares, but Many Don't Qualify for the New Low Rate," by Jeff D. Opdyke and Tom Herman, *Wall Street Journal*, August 19, 2003, D1.

[15] Code Sec. 1(h)(D)(i), as added by the 2001 Act and Code Sec. 163(d)(4)(B), as amended by the 2003 Act.

tax rates for qualifying dividends and the ordinary tax rates applicable to margin interest expense. Taxpayers, however, who lack excess investment income may still potentially benefit by borrowing through qualifying home equity loans. Benefits may be further enhanced by transferring funds, via gift, to a taxpayer who is in the five percent tax bracket.

    Example 1: Bob Bryant, a wealthy taxpayer, borrows $100,000, at a rate of 6 percent in order to invest in qualifying preferred stock, currently yielding 6 percent. Bob is subject to a marginal federal ordinary income tax rate of 35 percent, a federal dividends tax rate of 15 percent, and a state marginal tax rate of 5 percent. Bob invests his funds for one year.

Income generated	$100,000 @ 6%	$6,000	
Less taxes	$6,000 @ 20% [15% fed. + 5% st.]	1,200	
			$4,800
Interest expense	$100,000 @ 6%	$6,000	
Less tax benefit	$6,000 @ 40% [35% fed. + 5% st.]	2,400	
			3,600
Net benefit			$1,200

    Example 2: Same as Example 1, except that the borrowed $100,000 is transferred as a gift to Bob's daughter, Brenda, age 14, who is subject to a federal dividends tax rate of five percent and a state marginal tax rate of five percent.

Income generated	(same as #1)	$6,000	
Less taxes	$6,000 @ 10% [5% fed. + 5% st.]	600	
			$5,400
Net interest expense	(same as #1)		3,600
Net benefit			$1,800

Note that if Bob borrows funds at six percent/year subject to full deductibility, he needs to generate a pre-tax return of only about 3.9 percent in order to break even.

.05 Sunset Provisions and Benefit Changes

    The provisions providing reduced rates of taxation on dividends and capital gains are scheduled to expire for tax years beginning after December 31, 2008.[16] A zero-percent rate replaces the five-percent tax rate for tax years beginning after December 31, 2007 and ending with tax years beginning after December 31, 2008.[17]

    TAX PLANNING: The year 2008, assuming there is no subsequent change in the law, provides a unique opportunity for lower income taxpayers to recognize capital gains without being subject to federal income tax. A

---

[16] Act Sec. 303 of the 2003 Act.

[17] Code Sec. 1(h)(1)(B), as amended by the 2003 Act.

potential related benefit is that taxpayers may also be able to avoid state taxes in cases where the state tax is computed on the basis of federal income.

¶202 Individual Stocks—Best for Controlling Taxes, but Often Impractical

.01 Benefit–Shareholder Controls Timing of Recognition of Gain

The holding of individual stocks, rather than mutual funds, normally provides investors with the best opportunities to control and/or minimize the recognition of capital gains. Whereas mutual funds, including index funds and exchange-traded funds, may generate taxable capital gains from a variety of trading transactions (e.g., shareholder redemptions), individual stocks will normally not be subject to taxable gain until sale by their shareholder. Further, if a shareholder holds stock until death, taxable gain may, in many cases, be avoided entirely.[18]

.02 Detriments—Commission Costs and Portfolio Tracking Error

An initial deterrent for some investors considering investing in individual stocks will be the commission costs incurred upon purchase and sale. Even, however, where an investor can minimize transaction costs, by buying in large blocks and holding them for extensive periods of time, the difficulty of achieving sufficient diversification may preclude the use of individual shares as an option.

A study conducted by Ronald Surz and Michael Price found that a portfolio of fifteen well diversified stocks provided a tracking error (defined as one standard deviation away from the market) of 5.4 percent a year. If, for example, investment returns were 11 percent for the year, an investor should not have been very surprised to find his or her individual return to be as much as 16.4 percent or as little as 5.6 percent. A group of sixty well-diversified stocks brought the tracking error down to 3.5 percent, an amount that would still be too high for many investors.[19]

The following example shows how a range of just two percentage points, plus or minus, can impact an investor's return over a range of time periods.

> **Example 3:** Listed below are the investment returns for a $100,000 investment with an expected return of ten percent, plus or minus two percent, over periods of five, ten, and twenty years.

---

[18] Code Sec. 1022, as added by The Economic Growth and Tax Relief Reconciliation Act of 2001, eliminates the full tax-free step up in basis for property acquired from a decedent dying after December 31, 2009. Executors, however, will be able to increase the basis of estate property by up to $4,300,000 ($1,300,000 + $3,000,000 additional for a surviving spouse).

[19] "The Truth About Diversification by the Numbers," by R. Surz and M. Price, *Journal of Investing,* Winter 2000, Vol. 9, Issue 4, pp. 93-95.

Time Period	Rate of Return		
	8%	*10%*	*12%*
5 Years	$146,900	$161,100	$176,200
10 Years	$215,900	$259,400	$310,600
20 Years	$466,100	$672,800	$964,600

.03 Practical Limitation—Publicly Available Information May Be Misleading or Inadequate

An additional practical problem, beyond achieving diversification, is that there may be a lack of unbiased critical information available for evaluation of individual corporations. A mid-December 2000 review of analysts' recommendations, for example, found that only 2.1 percent were categorized as "sell," whereas 31.2 percent were "strong buys," and 39.9 percent were "buys."[20] After-the-fact information indicates that in most cases, the more appropriate types of recommendations would have been "sells" or "strong sells." S&P 500 performance was −9.1 percent and −11.9 percent in 2000 and 2001, respectively. Further complicating matters is that terminology used for ratings varies significantly between brokerage operations. According to Chuck Hill, research director at Thomson Financial/ First Call, "You have to have a decoder ring to know what ratings really mean."[21]

Individual investors who prefer to do their own research and avoid possible biases and/or misinterpretations of analysts' reports may, nonetheless, still be at a disadvantage because they often lack access to information that may be available to the professional prognosticators (e.g., interviews with management).

¶203 Mutual Funds—Provide a Variety of Planning Opportunities without Burdens of Individual Stock Ownership

Investors who find it too costly and/or too impractical to own individual shares of stock may consider the purchase of mutual funds. A principle benefit of mutual fund investing is that it allows investors to purchase ownership in a wide range of stocks without incurring separate commission costs for each individual item held in a fund's portfolio. Fees, however, are normally charged for expenses and, in some cases, loads (commissions) may be imposed upon purchases and/ or redemptions.

.01 Evaluating Passive and Managed Investment Approaches

Investors choosing the mutual fund route may need to evaluate the circumstances where a managed or passive (i.e., index-based) approach may be more likely to provide the best after-tax returns. The theoretical benefit of holding a managed mutual fund is that the fund manager will be able to generate a return that is superior to its benchmark (e.g., S&P 500 Index), after taking into account all fees and taxes. In practice, however, it is often difficult, particularly in taxable

---

[20] Results according to Thomson Financial/IBES, as reported in "Call It Courage: Bold Analysts Buck the Trend on Sell Ratings," by Robert McGough, *The Wall Street Journal Interactive Edition*," January 2, 2001.

[21] Quoted in "Analysts' Reports: Don't Buy the Hype," by Jeff D. Opdyke, *The Wall Street Journal*, July 10, 2001.

accounts, for managed accounts to generate pre-tax returns that are sufficiently superior to compensate for inherent cost disadvantages. The following sections of this chapter will explain:

1. How index-based funds may provide significant after-tax advantages,

2. The different methods for adopting index-based investing, and

3. Areas where index-based or the managed approach are potentially more likely to yield superior results.

¶204 Benefits of Index-Based Investing—Overview

The primary tax benefit for investors choosing index-based investments is the reduced passthrough of capital gains that result from a low turnover of investment holdings. While the average mutual fund has a high turnover rate,[22] often requiring a significant current passthrough of net capital gains to the shareholders, many index and exchange-traded funds have minimal or even no passthrough of capital gains and thereby provide opportunities for extensive deferral of gain recognition.

The benefits of index based investing are, however, not necessarily limited to taxable accounts. Benefits from reduced costs and opportunities for diversification may make index-based investments attractive choices for inclusion even in tax-deferred or tax-free accounts (e.g., Roth IRA). Since the client should, of course, be most concerned with after-tax returns, it may be beneficial for the adviser to delineate the circumstances where particular types of index-based investments may be most optimal.

.01 Turnover Rate, Even After JGTRRA, Can Significantly Affect Long-Term After-Tax Returns

Although JTGRRA eliminated the reduced capital gains rates for investments held more than five years, investors should still consider a fund's rate of turnover for their long-term investments. Over an extended period of time, a low-turnover index-based investment can potentially provide significant after-tax advantages over its managed counterpart, even where all of the managed fund's gains are taxable at preferred long-term rates.

Example 4: A managed fund has a turnover of 100 percent/year. All gains are recognized annually and subject to tax at a federal rate of 15 percent. Gains are also subject to a state and local income tax rate of 5 percent/year. Total annual tax rate=20 percent.

An index-based investment has a turnover rate of 0 percent/year. Gains are recognized only upon redemption, at which point they are subject to a total rate of 20 percent [15 percent federal rate + 5 percent state rate].

Initial investment in both cases is $100,000.

---

[22] The average turnover rate for a mutual fund was approximately 90 percent in 1999 per "How Mutual Funds Lost Their Way," by John C. Bogle, *Wall Street Journal,* June 20, 2000.

Scenario A – 8% Pre-tax rate of return
After-tax payout

Holding period	Index Investment	Managed Fund Investment
5 Years	$137,500	$136,400
10 Years	$192,700	$186,000
20 Years	$392,900	$345,800
30 Years	$825,000	$604,400

Scenario B – 12% Pre-tax rate of return
After-tax payout

Holding period	Index Investment	Managed Fund Investment
5 Years	$161,000	$158,100
10 Years	$268,500	$250,100
20 Years	$791,700	$625,500
30 Years	$2,418,900	$1,427,300

PRACTICE POINTER: The difficulty for the manager of a managed fund to match the after-tax performance of an index-based account is further exacerbated by the effect of additional expenses, such as management fees. Clients should be made aware, therefore, that substantially higher pre-tax returns might be required of a managed fund in order for it to meet or exceed the after-tax performance of low-turnover index-based investments.

.02 Additional Risks of Managed Funds—Manager Turnover and Market Impact Costs

Additional practical considerations for managed funds, beyond those of higher operating costs, include the potential risks to future fund performance from manager turnover and market impact costs. Alternatively, neither of these risks should prove to be very significant for index-based investments.

The average manager tenure for open-end mutual funds is only 4.4 years, according to *Morningstar*.[23] An investor who chooses a particular mutual fund, based on the performance of a fund manager, therefore, is at risk that expected fund performance may not continue should that manager depart. If that event should occur, the investor may need to choose between two unpleasant options:

1. Sell shares and prematurely recognize taxable capital gains, or

2. Hold shares and incur the risk that the new manager may not be as capable a performer.

A second consideration, assuming an investor is confident that a managed fund will generate superior returns, is the risk that the fund may, effectively, become a victim of its own success. Small funds that achieve success are often likely to draw in new investors, causing them to grow in size. A consequence of this growth, for example, may be that a fund that achieved superior returns by investing in small capitalization companies may become too large to do so

---

[23] "Tenure of Fund Managers," Ask the Expert, Conversation #926, Reply #1," *Morningstar.com*, December 8, 1999.

¶204.02

without incurring market impact costs (e.g., purchase of large blocks of stock causes the stock price to increase), and thereby lose its principal means of outperforming the market. While some open funds later do become closed to new investors, it may be difficult to predict at what point, if any, this would happen.

¶205 Forms of Index-Based Investing

There are essentially two means of index-based investing: mutual funds and exchange traded funds. Both forms of investing track selected indexes (e.g., S&P 500), sectors (e.g., technology), or countries. The optimal choice for an investor holding such investments in a taxable account will depend largely on the potential for passthrough of taxable gains, operating expenses, commission costs, and in the case of exchange traded shares, bid-ask spreads and liquidity.

.01 Index-Based Mutual Funds

Index-based funds vary from traditional mutual funds in that they do not employ managers to strategically select stocks for purposes of attempting to achieve optimal capital and/or income appreciation. Managers may, however, play a significant role in influencing the return of an index-based mutual fund through a variety of means. They may increase returns by more quickly reinvesting dividends, reducing trading costs, and employing the use of futures contracts instead of stocks, in cases where such contracts are trading at a discount. Managers, additionally, may affect tax-adjusted returns by adopting the specific identification method for stock sales and then selling the highest basis shares first. Returns may also vary because of differences in firm imposed operating expenses and in some cases, the imposition of a load charge.[24] In any event, clients and their advisers should *not* assume that future returns for all funds tracking an identical index will be the same.

Typical advantages of index-based mutual funds, as compared with exchange-traded funds, include commission-free purchase and redemption transactions, and a lack of bid-sell spread variations on redemptions. Probably the most common significant disadvantage of index-based mutual funds, as compared to exchange-traded funds, is a higher level of passthrough of capital gains. While these passthroughs may often be low relative to managed mutual funds, the amount of difference in passthrough may be substantive for some index-based accounts, especially for those that are not based on the S&P 500 Index.

.02 Exchange-Traded Funds

Conceptually, exchange traded funds are baskets of stocks that trade like individual shares. They are similar to index funds in that they are based on an underlying sector (e.g., S&P 500) and normally have low operating costs. They differ from index funds, however, in that they can be traded throughout the day and can be sold in a short position. Exchange-traded funds may be structured as

---

[24] These issues are discussed in more detail in "Index Funds: The Similarities are Different – Philosophies, Yields Vary Despite The Goal of Mirror-ing Market," by Bridget O'Brien, *The Wall Street Journal*, May 21, 1999.

unit investment trusts (UITs) or as special share classes of open-end mutual funds.

.03 Unit Investment Trusts

The unit investment trust (UIT) structure is the form that is employed by two of the most widely held exchange-traded funds: Nasdaq 100 Trust Shares (referred to as "Cubes," because of its QQQ ticker symbol) and Standard & Poor's Depository Receipts (referred to as "Spiders," because of its SPDR ticker symbol). Although the two funds have received widespread acceptance in the marketplace, all or almost all of the newer exchange traded funds are being issued in the open-end mutual fund structure.

A disadvantage of the UIT structure is a requirement that dividends can only be reinvested quarterly, rather than daily. Theoretically, such lag could potentially cause a significant drag on a fund's performance. Nonetheless, with dividend yields commonly in the annual range of 1 percent or less and with UITs typically reinvesting dividends in interest bearing accounts, the loss of earnings may not be large enough to deter many investors. If, however, dividend rates are or become high, the reinvestment lag may become more of a concern.

¶206 Passthrough of Gains—Comparing Managed Funds, Index Funds, and Exchange-Traded Funds

In comparing the potential for passthrough of gains for a taxable account, managed funds, in general, hold the highest risk exposure, while exchange-traded funds normally hold the least.

Managed funds, in general, hold the risk of being subject to the passthrough of taxable gains resulting from three types of transactions:

1. Sales incurred to meet shareholder redemptions,
2. Sales incurred pursuant to an active trading strategy, and
3. Sales incurred to keep a portfolio within its stated goals (e.g., small capitalization growth companies).

Index funds, generally, are subject to the risk of the passthrough of gains from:

1. Sales incurred to meet shareholder redemptions, and
2. Sales incurred to adjust their portfolio following a periodic reconfiguration of an index (e.g., annual change in companies included in the S&P 500).

Exchange traded funds typically have the lowest risk of potential passthrough of gains. The amount passed through, for most funds, has been minimal or nonexistent and results normally just from the reconfiguration of their underlying indexes. Exchange-traded funds minimize passthroughs of gains on redemptions by returning actual shares of stock, rather than cash, to their large investors.

¶205.03

An additional risk for country specific investments is the regulated investment company requirement that a fund may hold no more than 25 percent of the value of total assets in the securities of any one issuer at the close of any quarter.[25] Theoretically, this rule could also apply in a domestic setting, but is much more likely to apply in situations where there are one or two dominant companies, as may be the case in some non-U.S. countries.

.01 Shareholder Redemptions—Passthrough of Gains

Investors in both managed funds and index funds face the risk of passthrough of gains from redemptions. The risk of this passthrough may vary depending upon the size of a fund's built-in gains and the manager's opportunities to fulfill shareholder redemptions through the sale of high basis shares. Managers of managed funds also have the opportunity to mitigate the passthrough of gains through altering their portfolio, by selling at losses selected shares of stock that have declined in value.

If a fund's redemptions are relatively consistent from year to year there may be less likelihood of taxable transactions arising from redemption related sales in a particular year. If, however, a fund experiences much larger than average redemptions it could, theoretically, be forced to deplete all of its higher basis shares and then sell the lower basis shares requiring significant passthroughs of gains to the fund's shareholders. In practice, however, it may be that if unusually large redemptions were to occur, it would be in tandem with a decline in the value of the fund's shares that, in turn, would decrease the likelihood of a large-scale passthrough of gains.

.02 Management Directed Sale—Passthrough of Gains

An additional risk for holders of managed funds, not faced by index fund shareholders, is the passthrough of taxable gains resulting from management directed sales. Investors evaluating the risk of passthrough of taxable gains for a managed fund should consider not only the amount of built-in gain, but also its expected annual turnover and the manager's trading style.

An example of this risk was a major capital gain distribution of the Brandywine Fund that resulted largely from a reduction in the fund's technical sector from 60 percent to 27 percent.[26] While some managed funds are more tightly restricted in terms of their investment choices (e.g., large capitalization manufacturing companies), this fund provides its managers with broad latitude to invest and switch amongst a variety of sectors. Largely as a result of this shift in investing strategy, investors, including those who purchased in the second half of the year and realized no economic gains, were forced to recognize significant capital gains.[27]

---

[25] Code Sec. 851(b).

[26] Reported in "Capital Gains Payouts Hit Investors Early," by Karen Damato and Ken Brown, *The Wall Street Journal*, August 25, 2000, C1.

[27] Investors who held this fund throughout the year in a tax-deferred or tax-exempt account, however, were probably overall satisfied with its performance, because it was one of a minority that generated net economic gains in 2000.

.03 Changes in Indexes—Passthrough of Gains

Index funds have the risk of mandated passthrough of gains resulting from their periodic reconfiguration, a risk that normally does not strictly exist with managed funds. If, for example, the composition of the S&P 500 changes, then an S&P 500 index fund will be required to sell the stocks that have been removed from the index and purchase the ones that have been added. Managed funds, by contrast, will normally not be required to make such changes. Nonetheless, if a fund is marketed as investing in a particular sector (e.g., large capitalization technology), management may feel compelled to dispose of stocks that no longer fall within the fund's investment objectives (e.g., a company within the company's existing portfolio changes in size and/or business operations).

Older more established funds may have larger amounts of built-in gains than ones that have been more recently established. Very new funds, however, may be at risk of having to pass through gains as short-term, in cases where they do not have sufficient number of shares that have been held for more than one year.

.04 Regulated Investment Companies' 25 Percent Rule— Passthrough of Gains

Funds tracking individual countries or sectors where one or two companies dominate, may provide a heightened risk of passthrough of gains resulting from application of the Code Section 851(b) rule that provides that a regulated investment company may have no more than 25 percent in value of its total assets invested in any one company. In the year 2000, for example, iShares MSCI Canada and iShares MSCI exchange-traded funds paid cash dividends equal to 23 percent and 18 percent of their prices a week earlier, before they went ex-dividend. These passthroughs were largely a result of required sales of companies that grew above the 25 percent size threshold, Nortel Networks Corp. and L.M. Ericsson Telephone Co., respectively.[28]

¶207 Evaluating Index Funds for Inclusion in Taxable or Tax-Exempt and/or Tax-Deferred Accounts

.01 S&P 500 Index

Funds based on the S&P 500 Index typically incur relatively small changes resulting from its annual reconfiguration. Unlike indexes such as the Russell 2000 and Russell 1000, where the component stocks are determined strictly by size, the S&P 500 Index's portfolio is selected by a committee. Historically, the committee has made only minor annual adjustments to the index and, as a result, the annual turnover rates for S&P 500 based index funds have been minimal. Generally, if some funds are to be held in a taxable account, an S&P 500 based fund may be a good choice because of the potential for a very low turnover rate.

---

[28] As reported in "Junk Bond Prices Link to Fund Lessens," by Dena Aubin, *The Wall Street Journal*, August 30, 2000.

.02 Russell Indexes (Russell 3,000, Russell 2,000, and Russell 1,000) and the S&P SmallCap 600 Index

An investor who is considering investing in a Russell 3000 based fund may potentially reduce taxes by segmenting his holdings into Russell 1000 based and Russell 2000 based holdings. The investor may benefit by holding a Russell 2000 based fund in a tax-exempt or tax-deferred account ahead of a Russell 1000 based fund, because Russell 2000 based funds may have inherently greater possibilities of generating passthroughs of capital gains. While funds may be dropped from the annual reconfiguration of the Russell 2000 by becoming either too large or too small, funds dropped from the Russell 1000 may be dropped only for becoming too small. Assuming that companies that have declined in size are less likely to generate gains, then the Russell 1000 based funds may provide a greater possibility for minimization of passthrough of capital gains.

TAX PLANNING: A small capitalization alternative to a Russell 2000 based fund, potentially providing reduced levels of turnover and, therefore, greater opportunities for tax deferral, would be a fund based on the S&P SmallCap 600. While the SmallCap 600 tracks a more limited group of stocks, some investors may deem its breadth sufficient for tracking the small capitalization market.

Distinguishing characteristics of the SmallCap 600, other than its smaller set stock set, are:

1. Lower turnover potential because it is reconfigured only once each year, and

2. Less speculative character, because stocks are selected for inclusion by a committee; the subcommittee typically does not include companies with short operating histories.

.03 Growth vs. Value Indexes

Value funds may generate slightly higher current taxable income than growth funds because of higher dividends. The tax benefits of indexing by growth/value criteria may be limited however, because the difference in dividend yields may be relatively small and the turnover required for annual reconfiguration may be relatively high.

Attempts to further bifurcate the market, through sorting by both size *and* style, may not necessarily yield better results because of mandated annual reconfigurations and resulting high turnover. Small capitalization growth index funds based on the S&P Small Cap 600/Barra Growth Index, for example, may have turnover rates nearly as high as the average managed fund.

PRACTICE POINTER: A more important consideration for many investors than maximum tax deferral may be to reduce volatility by holding both growth and value stocks. During the five year period which ended September 30, 2001, for example, the total returns for growth and value funds was almost identical: S&P 500/BARRA Growth Index: 9.94 percent and S&P 500/BARRA Value Index: 9.8 percent, while results in some individual years varied sharply:

Growth, 2000: -22%, 1999: +28%; Value: 2000: +6%, 1999: +13%.

A practical consideration is whether, in difficult financial times, an investor is prepared to stay committed to a long-term "buy and hold" strategy. While a strategy of holding 100 percent growth stocks may provide the opportunity to generate a slightly higher proportion of income through capital gains, it may well be that the taxpayer who holds a more diversified portfolio is more likely to actually execute a "buy and hold" strategy in turbulent financial circumstances.

¶208 Choosing Index vs. Managed Funds

Index-based funds typically, as discussed, have inherent advantages of low turnover, reducing current passthrough of taxable gains, and low expenses, increasing pre-tax returns. Index funds, however, lack the potential to benefit from a manager's expertise in deciding which stocks to buy and sell for a portfolio. If a client is attempting to evaluate whether to purchase a passive or a managed fund, three factors may be helpful in determining which type of fund would be most appropriate:

1. Managed fund's R-squared correlation,
2. Size of the stocks within the fund, and
3. U.S./International composition.

.01 R-Squared

R-squared is the technical term used to describe the mutual association between two factors. In cases of investing, it is not unusual for a managed mutual fund to have a high R-squared score when compared with a specific index. Funds that have very high R-squared scores are sometimes referred to as "closet indexers." In some cases, funds will be marketed as "enhanced index funds," with the objective being to provide a return that is slightly higher than a designated index.

In general, it is difficult for a managed fund possessing a high R-squared to outperform a passive fund, because the manager must provide performance superior enough to overcome the cost of management, while independently managing only a small percentage of the portfolio.

Example 5: Peter Dow invests $100,000 in a fund having an R-squared score of 90 relative to the underlying benchmark. The fund's annual operating expenses are 1.5 percent, while the costs for a comparable index fund are 0.5 percent. The total expenses for the managed fund, therefore, are $1,500 for the year, as opposed to $500 for the index fund. Since the correlation is 90 percent, effectively there is only $10,000 (10 percent of $100,000) in assets that are available to be managed by the manager.

The index fund is assumed to earn a return of ten percent/year before expenses and taxes. The managed fund is also assumed to earn that return on the correlated portion (90 percent of fund's investments).

Index fund net pre-tax return	
Investment income [$100,000 x 10%]	$10,000
Expenses [$100,000 x 0.5%]	500
Net pre-tax return	$ 9,500

Return required on actively managed portion of managed fund in order to match performance of the index fund

Net pre-tax return of index fund	$9,500
Return on correlated portion	
[$100,000 x 90% x 10%]	$9,000
Expenses [$100,000 x 1.5%]	1,500
	7,500
Return required on uncorrelated portion	$2,000 (20%)

In this example, the uncorrelated portion of the managed fund must provide a return of 20 percent, double the amount of return that is generated by the index portion, merely to match the index fund's overall return. In situations such as this one, where there is a high R-squared score, investors may determine that it is highly unlikely that the manager could generate the required superior return and, as a result, opt for the index fund even for holdings in a tax-exempt or tax-deferred account.

> **PRACTICE POINTER:** In practice, the performance of the managed fund may need to be even higher than that shown in the example, because:
>
> 1. Managed funds typically have higher cash balances than index funds, reducing the amount available for stock investment, and
>
> 2. Managers may be attempting to generate the higher required income through short-term trading, resulting in higher transaction costs and also, possibly, higher proportions of income taxed at ordinary income rates.

.02 Index Funds May Provide Best Opportunities in the Large Capitalization Sector

Passive vs. managed—the effect of company sizes within the portfolio. If an investor chooses to assemble a portfolio comprised of both managed and passive funds, the best choice for holding index funds may be in the large growth sector. A study conducted by *Morningstar* found that only two percent of managed large growth funds beat the Wilshire Large Growth Index for the five-year period ending July 31, 1998. Managed funds were shown to fare better in the small stock sector where they outperformed their passive counterparts approximately half the time. A reason theorized for the finding is that it is easier for an analyst to uncover information about small companies than for large companies.[29]

---

[29] "Indexing Shines in New Morningstar Study," by Susan Dzibinski, *Morningstar.com*, September 15, 1998. The difficulty in achieving a research edge for large corporations is illustrated, for example, by the

TAX PLANNING: Opportunities to invest in the large capitalization sector and also to achieve high tax efficiency may exist through investments indexed to the S&P 500 and/or the Russell 1000 Index. The S&P 500 Index, whose composition is determined by a committee, has historically had very low turnover. The Russell 1000 Index, whose components are determined strictly by size, may have the benefit of mandated sales being primarily of less successful companies, companies that no longer meet the index's size criteria. As a result, the companies that are dropped may be less likely to have increased significantly in value and, therefore, may generate less passthroughs of capital gains.

Passive vs. managed—international investing. A potential difficulty for investors attempting to evaluate the relative performance of managed vs. passive funds in the international area is that existing indexes may not closely mirror the global economy. As a result, performance comparisons may be skewed, depending more upon the composition of an index than the skill of management. The Morgan Stanley Europe, Australia and Far East Index (EAFE), for example, for many years heavily weighted its composition towards the Japanese sector. As a result, the EAFE index would generally outperform managed international funds in years where Japanese stocks did well, but underperform it in years where they did poorly. Investors may achieve better comparability in performance by comparing single country index funds with single country managed funds. Investing in single country funds, however, may make it more difficult to achieve the goal of a globally diversified portfolio.

Evaluating exchange-traded funds for inclusion in taxable and/or tax-deferred accounts. Exchange-traded funds while, in general, providing very low passthroughs of taxable gains may, in some cases, provide a more than minimal likelihood of such occurrence and, thereby, make them less attractive choices for inclusion in a taxable account. These circumstances include:

1. The fund's portfolio includes holdings of individual companies that are near the 25 percent quarterly limit, that if exceeded, would require their sale by the end of period (Code Sec. 851(b)). These risks may be more pronounced in exchange-traded funds for individual countries where there may be one or two dominant companies.

2. The fund is relatively new. A fund that has been recently established and is experiencing rapid growth may not be able to offset gains with losses because of the application of the wash sale rules. In the case of iShares S&P 500 Index, the fund grew so quickly in its initial year of operation, 2000, that it was unable to use some tax losses because a very large amount of in-kind contributions were received within the wash sale period.

(Footnote Continued)

fact that Microsoft is tracked by thirty analysts, whereas GenCorp, a $1 billion (sales) corporation is tracked by only one analyst. Information is according to Thomson Financial/IBES, as reported in "Wallflowers," by Brett D. Helgren, *Forbes*, June 11, 2001, p. 194.

¶209 Choosing Index vs. Exchange-Traded Funds

An investor deciding whether to invest in a particular index-fund or its exchange-traded counterpart should consider a variety of factors, including the following:

1. **Annual operating expenses.** Index funds and exchange-traded funds tracking an identical index (e.g., S&P 500) may have significantly different operating expenses. Frequently, but not always, the expenses for the exchange-traded funds are lower than for similar index funds.

2. **Capital gains passthrough for taxable accounts.** Frequently, but not always, the passthrough of capital gains are lower for exchange-traded shares than for comparable index funds.

3. **Transaction costs.** Most, but not all index funds can be purchased without incurring a load (commission charge). Exchange-traded funds, however, normally require the incurring of commission charges for both purchases and sales. In general, if the expenses of an exchange-traded fund are lower than that for a comparable index fund, then purchases of the exchange-traded funds may be more optimal where the shares are bought in large blocks and economies of scale can be achieved. Alternatively, if a shareholder is making small incremental investments each month, then the commission costs for purchasing may outweigh the benefits of lower annual expenses. A related factor is the expected holding period. The longer the holding period, the less the commission cost becomes a factor relative to annual operating expenses.

4. **ETFs.** Spread between ETF trading price and underlying value of stocks. A potential risk for exchange-traded funds, not existing for index funds, is that the ETF may sell at a discount to the underlying value of its component stocks. ETFs that have high trading volume may be expected to generate small and perhaps even insignificant variations between their trading prices and the value of the underlying stock components. Alternatively, where volume is low, arbitrageurs may move slowly in correcting variations.

5. **ETFs.** Bid/ask spread–Bid-ask spreads may be significant in cases where there is little trading. Further, if an investor seeks to dispose of a large segment of exchange traded funds in a thinly traded market, she may incur market impact costs, whereby the selling price decreases as the size of the sale unit increases.

6. **ETFs.** Unit Investment Trust vs. Mutual Fund Structure–Generally, only older exchange traded funds are structured using the unit investment trust structure. The primary disadvantage of this form is that it allows for reinvestment of dividends only on a quarterly, rather than an immediate basis.

Example 6: *Conceptual*—Maggie Jones is considering making a large one-time long-term investment in the technology sector for her taxable account. A widely traded exchange-traded fund may be purchased which offers the benefits of lower annual expenses and lower expected pass-through of capital gains. The fund, being widely traded, provides only minimal risk of significant bid-ask spreads and variations between its trading price and the underlying stocks' value.

In this case, the exchange trade fund might be expected to be superior for the taxable account for the following reasons:

     a. Annual expenses are lower,

     b. Commissions, while providing a cost not required in a no-load mutual fund, may be small relative to the size and holding period of the investment, and

     c. ETF related risks are low for: 1) discounted price of fund relative to its underlying share; and 2) bid/ask spread on sale.

     Example 7: *Quantitative*—Robert Ritazza is considering making periodic purchases, $1,000/month of an index-based investment specializing in emerging market ventures. Investments are to be held for an average of four years. Investments are assumed to earn 12 percent/year with no ordinary income.

Exchange-traded fund

Commission costs—$25 for each purchase and sale
Annual expenses—0.30 %
Expected annual recognition of capital gains—0% (expected state and local tax rate of 20% upon redemption)

Index fund

Commission costs—$0
Annual expenses—0.60%
Expected annual recognition of capital gains—20% (expected state and local tax rate of 20% upon redemption)

Exchange-traded fund—Single $1,000 Investment

	Year 1	Year 2	Year 3	Year 4
Investment—beg. of year	$1,000	$1,089	$1,216	$1,358
Commission	(25)	(0)	(0)	(25)
	975	1,089	1,216	1,333
Income—12%	117	131	146	160
	1,092	1,220	1,362	1,493
Operating expenses	(3)	(4)	(4)	(4)
	1,089	1,216	1,358	1,489
Capital gain taxes	(0)	(0)	(0)	(98)
End of year	$1,089	$1,216	$1,358	$1,391

Capital gains tax computation—year of sale:

Sales price $1,489 - $1,000 = $489 x .20 = $98

¶209

Index Fund—Single $1,000 Investment

	Year 1	Year 2	Year 3	Year 4
Investment—beg. of year	$1,000	$1,108	$1,229	$1,363
Commission	0	0	0	0
	1,000	1,108	1,229	1,363
Income—12%	120	133	147	146
	1,120	1,241	1,376	1,527
Operating expenses	(7)	(7)	(8)	(9)
	1,113	1,234	1,368	1,518
Capital gain taxes	(5)	(5)	(5)	(89)
End of year	$1,108	$1,229	$1,363	$1,429

Capital gains computation—year of sale

Purchase basis	$1,000
Increases—gain recognized	
Year 1: $113 x .2	23
Year 2: $121 x .2	24
Year 3: $134 x .2	27
Basis for sale	$1,074

Capital Gains Taxes—Year 4

Sales price $1,518 – 1,074 = $444 x .20 = $89

The index fund, in this example, provides a superior return in each of the four years. If, however, any one of the following conditions were present then the exchange-traded fund might have provided superior returns

1. **Higher purchase amount.** As the dollar amount of the investment increases, the higher passthrough of capital gains for the index fund and higher operating expenses may outweigh the ETF's commission costs. After JGTRRA, the effect of current passthroughs of capital gains is somewhat lessened as the federal tax rate for capital gains has been reduced from 20 percent to 15 percent for most investors.

2. **Longer holding period.** As the time period increases, the higher pass-through of capital gains for the index fund may also outweigh the ETF's commission costs.

3. **Lower transaction costs.** On-line trading or other forms of discount trading may reduce the ETF's transaction cost detriment.

¶210 Funds with Loss Carryovers Create Tax Deferral Opportunities for New Investors

Previously nondeductible losses incurred by funds may create opportunities for new investors, by allowing them to reap the benefits of loss carryovers, despite nonowner status during the loss period. This benefit arises from regulations that prevent regulated investment companies from passing current net capital losses through to existing shareholders. Instead, these regulations require regulated investment companies,[30] sustaining net capital losses, to carry them forward to each of the next eight years following the loss year.[31]

While the application of these provisions is generally disadvantageous to existing shareholders who cannot currently deduct losses, it does create opportunities for new shareholders to generate tax-deferred trading income through offsets of a fund's trading gains with prior trading losses. Only when the mutual fund shares are sold would the taxpayer be subject to gain recognition on the appreciation of the underlying investments. If the funds are held until death, the realized but unrecognized gains from the tax-deferral period may escape taxation altogether.

¶211 Gain Lock-Ins—Short Sales of Exchange-Traded Funds

The use of short sales of exchange-traded shares to effectively achieve a lock-in of gains is a technique popularly used by managers of hedge funds[32] that also can work well for individual investors. Although investors are precluded from achieving a full deferral of gain by Section 1259's prohibition of use of offsetting "substantially identical" securities, opportunities may be available through the use of exchange-traded funds to achieve lock-ins that are significant enough to reduce market risk to a satisfactory minimum.

A distinguishing characteristic of exchange-traded funds is that, unlike traditional mutual funds, they can be used in short sale transactions. Therefore, if an investor is considering a fund investment with an eye towards achieving a future lock-in of gains, then a traditional mutual fund should be purchased first, because only the ETF can be used for the offsetting short sale.

Scenario A

Tommy Rich has $100,000 invested in an "enhanced" mutual fund tracking small growth stocks. In the last three months the value of the fund has increased from $60,000 to $100,000. Mr. Rich believes that now is a prudent time to shift out of this investment, but does not want to pay taxes at ordinary income rates nor take the risk of waiting nine months for the fund to achieve long-term capital gain status. Mr. Rich could potentially lock in a substantial portion of his gain by selling short an exchange-traded fund having a portfolio of very similar investments. While Mr. Rich cannot achieve 100 percent lock-in, the portion that is secure may be sufficient to satisfy him.

Scenario B

Mary Wealth's investments have yielded the same performance as that of the taxpayer in scenario A, but through an exchange-traded fund. If Mary wishes to substantially lock in gain she will not be able to do so through the short sale of a mutual fund, because they may not be sold in short transactions. While Mary may potentially achieve a reasonable lock-in of gains through other means (e.g., other exchange traded shares or "collar" transactions), her opportunities to do so may be significantly less than those available to the taxpayer in scenario A.

---

[30] As defined in Code Sec. 851.

[31] Reg. § 1.1212-1(a)(3)(g).

[32] "Exchange-Traded Funds Find Success Among Hedge Funds," by Allison Bisbey Colter, *The Wall Street Journal Interactive Edition,* July 12, 2001.

.01 "Substantially Identical"—An Ambiguous and Unsettled Issue

Investors should note that at this point there are no rulings or court decisions indicating what constitutes "substantially identical" for purposes of offsetting transactions between mutual funds and exchange-traded shares. While arguments could be made that funds or exchange-traded funds tracking the same index (e.g., S&P 500) are not substantially identical because of differences in management techniques (e.g., use of futures contracts instead of actual shares), a more conservative approach may be to employ passive funds (e.g., index funds) and limited management funds (e.g., enhanced index funds) as offsets against each other for purposes of achieving lock-ins of gains.

¶212 Tax-Managed Funds—An Alternative for Tax Efficient Investing

A viable alternative to index funds for tax-efficient investing, particularly with respect to small capitalization companies, may be tax-managed mutual funds. Tax-managed mutual funds may achieve high tax efficiency in a variety of ways including the following:

1. Managers focus on long-term investing, minimizing the requirement for passthroughs of capital gains.

2. Managers, if using a benchmark, use one that is likely to have a lower rate of turnover (e.g., use of S&P SmallCap 600 instead of the Russell 2000).

3. Managers employ a HIFO (highest in, first out) method of trading. Managers may also attempt to engage in loss harvesting, whereby stocks that have declined in value are sold.

4. Penalties are imposed on certain redemptions. The objective of imposing penalties is to discourage frequent and/or large redemptions that could cause the fund manager to sell stock.

5. Hedging strategies are used as alternatives to selling stocks with gains.

6. Growth stocks are favored over value stocks because they generate lower dividends. Investors in evaluating tax-managed funds should be careful to examine the holdings of the fund to ensure that they are providing the desired style mix.

Potential disadvantages of tax-managed funds:

1. The manager's ability to trade may be constrained, leading to lower pre-tax earnings.

2. Expenses may be higher than for a comparable index-based investment.

3. Potential exposure to built-in gains may increase over time. A more established fund, with a proven track record, may have significant higher risk of built-in gain passthroughs than more recently established funds.

4. Hedging strategies used to protect gains may not remain successful and could ultimately lead to losses.

¶212

TAX PLANNING: While tax-managed funds are available for a range of company sizes and investment styles, they may be most advantageous in the small capitalization area, where the tax benefits of index investing are often limited because of the higher turnover often associated with that sector.

¶213 Wash Sales Rules—Planning Opportunities with Mutual Funds

Investors who sell stock or mutual funds at a loss but replace it with a substantially identical item within a period of thirty days before or after the sale will have the loss disallowed, under the provisions of the wash sales rules.[33] These provisions do not apply to gains.

.01 Replacement of Index Funds with "Closet Indexers" May Provide Opportunities to Effectively Maintain Holdings While Deducting Losses

Opportunities to recognize current losses without substantive divestitures may be possible through sale and replacement of similar, but not "substantially identical" funds. One possible means of achieving this objective would be to sell an index fund at a loss and replace it with a highly correlated managed fund.

Example 8: Sally Casher sells her S&P 500 Index Fund for $100,000 and incurs a $15,000 loss. She immediately purchases a managed fund having an R-squared of 95. She may be able to deduct the full amount of loss, subject to annual limitations, while effectively only putting $5,000 at risk (5 percent of $100,000). If Sally prefers to be invested in the S&P fund, she could sell the managed fund and repurchase the S&P 500 Index Fund immediately after the 30-day wash period has expired.

Investors should be cautioned, however, that at least until there are rulings, regulations, or court decisions issued, it is possible that the courts and/or the I.R.S. could rule that funds, even if separately labeled as being index or managed, are substantially identical. Alternatively, it is possible that rulings could be issued indicating that funds tracking the same index, but not issued by the same company, are not substantially identical because of factors such as differences in fund operations (e.g., use of futures contracts) and/or shareholder exposure to built-in gains.

.02 Sale and Immediate Repurchase May Provide Opportunities to Benefit from Lower Tax Rates

The wash sale rules do *not* apply to gains and, therefore, may allow opportunities to minimize taxes through sale and immediate repurchase transactions, which would not be recognized in loss situations. The benefit of recognizing gains prematurely would be to take advantage of the 5 percent tax rate for lower income taxpayers.

---

[33] Code Sec. 1091.

Example 9: *Assumptions*—Richard Dupree purchased an investment in 1998 for $25,000. The investment has and is expected to continue to appreciate at a rate of 10 percent/year. The individual's ordinary income tax bracket is 15 percent in 2003 and is expected to increase to at least 30 percent for the next year and the foreseeable future.

Scenario A

Investment is held for ten years and then sold in 2008. Capital gains taxes of 15 percent are paid upon disposition.

Sales price (2008)	$64,850	
Taxes	(5,978)	[($64,850 - $25,000) x .15]
Net proceeds	$58,872	

Scenario B

Investment is held for five years and sold at its current value of $40,263. Taxes of $763 [($40,263 - $25,000) x .05] are paid at the time of the sale and the remaining proceeds, $39,500, are reinvested. After an additional five years the investment is sold at its current market value of $63,615.

Sales price (2008)	$63,615	
Taxes (2008)	(3,617)	[($63,615 – $39,500) x .15]
Taxes (2003)	(763)	($40,263 – $25,000) x .05]
	$59,235	

The total after tax-benefit from a simple repurchase and sale was $363 [$59,235 - $58,872].

TAX PLANNING: This technique may be particularly beneficial for individuals such as graduating students, who qualify for the five percent bracket in the current year, but expect to be ineligible to use it in future years.

TAX PLANNING: The technique of selling and repurchasing will be most advantageous in 2008, at which point qualifying taxpayers can benefit from a zero percent rate for capital gains. An additional benefit, for taxpayers who live in states where taxable income is based on federal amounts, is that the income may also be exempt for state income tax purposes.

In order to maximize this benefit, taxpayers who believe they will qualify for this reduced rate may wish to plan on maximizing sales in 2008, then working backwards to earlier years. In 2009, the capital gains rates are scheduled to revert to the pre-JGTRRA rates.

¶214 Small Business Stock—Opportunities to Exclude 50 Percent of Long-Term Capital Gain

Opportunities to exclude 50 percent of long-term capital gain may be available for individuals who become initial holders of stock in qualified small business corporations.[34] In order to qualify for this exclusion the corporation must

---

[34] The exclusion is increased to 60 percent in the case of the sale or exchange of stock of an enterprise business as defined in Code Sec. 1397C(a) that operates within an empowerment zone and was ac-

meet the criteria for categorization as a qualifying small business and the stock must be held for at least five years. Although in some cases the five-year holding period requirement may be viewed as a detriment, it does provide the opportunity to potentially have capital gains taxed at an effective rate of only 7.5 percent (15%/2) or even 2.5 percent (5%/2). The total amount excluded per issuer cannot exceed the *greater* of $10,000,000 ($5,000,000 for married individuals filing separately) or ten times the investor's basis in the stock, determined without regard to any addition after its original date of issue. The effective amount of this gain may also be reduced by application of the alternative minimum tax.

.01 Qualifying Small Business Stock

In order to qualify as small business stock the following requirements must be met:

1. Stock must be issued by a domestic C Corporation after August 10, 1993,[35]

2. Stock must be issued to the taxpayer directly or through an underwriter in exchange for money, property (not including stock), or compensation for services provided to the issuing corporation,[36]

3. At least 80 percent, by value, of the assets of the corporation are used in a qualifying trade or business,[37] and

4. Aggregate gross assets do not exceed $50,000,000 at the date of issuance.[38]

.02 Alternative Minimum Tax

The full exclusion benefit may be limited because of the requirement that seven percent of the 50-percent exclusion is treated as a tax preference item when computing AMTI.[39] Prior to the passage of JGTRRA, however, 42 percent of the exclusion (28 percent for stock acquired after 2000) was a preference item. These amounts are scheduled to again apply to tax years beginning after December 31, 2008.

.03 Gain May Be Deferred through Rollover into Other Qualified Stock[40]

Gain from the sale of small business stock may be deferred in cases where the proceeds from the sale are rolled over into other qualifying small business stock within sixty days. In order to qualify for this benefit, the original stock must be held for only six months. If there is a partial rollover, deferral applies only to the amount that is reinvested. Gain deferred is taken as a reduction in the basis of the replacement stock.

(Footnote Continued)

quired after December 31, 2000 (Code Sec. 1202(a)(2)).

[35] Code Sec. 1202(c)(1), (d)(1).

[36] Code Sec. 1202(c)(1).

[37] Code Sec. 1202(c)(2), (e).

[38] Code Sec. 1202(c)(1)(A), (d).

[39] Code Sec. 57(a)(7) as amended by the Jobs and Growth Tax Relief Reconciliation Act of 2003.

[40] Code Sec. 1045.

¶215 Small Business Stock—Opportunities to Deduct Losses Beyond $3,000

Investors considering investing in small business ventures but who are concerned about incurring nondeductible losses may gain some protection by becoming qualified purchasers of Section 1244 stock. Married taxpayers may claim as ordinary losses up to $100,000 per year, while other taxpayers may claim as ordinary losses a maximum of $50,000 per year.

Requirements to qualify for losses on small business stock are more restrictive than those applicable for the exclusion of gain. Whereas, for example, an investor who has acquired stock for services may be eligible for gain exclusion, he would not be eligible for the expanded allowances of losses. Additionally, the restriction that stock and paid-in surplus be limited to $1,000,000 may effectively preclude a company from acquiring the maximum of $50,000,000 in assets allowable for gain exclusion purposes.

.01 Claiming Ordinary Losses Beyond the $100,000 ($50,000) Annual Limitation

Although investors are only allowed to claim a maximum loss of $50,000 ($100,000 for spouses filing a joint return) in any one year, there is no restriction on selling shares over a period of years in order to maximize the loss allowance. Examples 10 and 11 compare the results of selling shares in one or two years.

> **Example 10:** Alice Lee, a married individual, sells her Section 1244 stock December 1, 2003, and incurs a $200,000 loss. The first $100,000 is treated as ordinary loss and the remaining $100,000 is treated as a loss from the sale of a capital asset. If there are no offsetting capital gains, only $3,000 of the capital loss will be allowed currently and the remaining amount would be carried forward indefinitely.

> **Example 11:** Same as in Example 10, except that 51 percent of the stock is sold December 1, 2003, providing the new owner with immediate effective control, and 49 percent is sold January 1, 2004. In 2003, $100,000 is treated as ordinary loss and $2,000 is treated as capital loss. In 2004, the remaining $98,000 would be treated as ordinary loss.

Note that in these examples it is immaterial as to whether the stock is individually or jointly owned. In order to qualify for the $100,000 per year exclusion it is only required that the husband and wife file a joint return.[41]

¶216 Small Business Stock—Planning to Ensure Eligibility for Both Gain and Loss Benefits

An investor's concerns with potential gain exclusion and/or potential for loss allowance may vary depending upon his or her individual situation. If, for example, an individual has a portfolio with significant items of built-in gain, the expanded loss allowance provided under Section 1244 may not provide an

---

[41] Code Sec. 1244(b).

incentive for acquiring an asset that meets its provisions. Alternatively, if an investor believes that a new venture has potential to do exceptionally well, that investment may be favored over another even where it does not provide the potential for gain exclusion under Section 1202. The reduced rates already applicable for capital gains (e.g., 20 percent or 18 percent) may provide sufficient incentive to invest in a particular venture.

In cases where there is potential for flexibility, however, the optimal situation may be to invest in a venture that meets the requirements for both gain exclusion and loss allowance. An investor who finds such an investment may be willing to take on more risk than for an investment that lacks both potential upside and downside benefits. In order to qualify for *both* sets of benefits the following requirements must be met:

1. Stock must be issued directly to the shareholder (or through a partnership of which the shareholder is a partner),[42]

2. Stock must be in a domestic corporation,[43]

3. Stock must have been issued for money or property (stock, securities, and services not allowable),[44]

4. Capital and paid-in surplus, at time of issuance, may not exceed $1,000,000,[45]

5. At least 80 percent, by value, of the company's assets must be used in a trade or business other than those engaged in professional services (e.g., law), financial services (e.g., banking), hospitality (e.g., hotels), farming, and mining and oil and gas production, and[46]

6. No more than 50 percent of the gross receipts during the five years prior to the year of sale may be from passive sources.[47]

The following example contains scenarios illustrating potential upside and downside benefits for an investment that qualifies for both Section 1244 gain and Section 1202 loss provisions.

Example 12: Bob Bennett, a married individual, purchases qualifying Section 1244 stock on January 1, 2003 for $300,000.

Scenario A

The stock is sold on January 8, 2008 for $600,000. Bob is allowed to exclude $150,000, 50 percent of the realized gain. His effective tax rate on the transaction is 7.5 percent (15%/2), assuming that the alternative minimum tax does apply.

Scenario B

The stock is sold on December 10, 2003 for $500,000. On January 31, 2004, Bob reinvests the entire proceeds into the stock of a replacement corporation. On January 8, 2008, he sells the proceeds of the replacement corporation for $10,000,000. All $9,700,000 qualifies for the 50 percent exclusion of gain even

---

[42] Reg. §1.1244(a)-1.
[43] Code Sec. 1202(c)(1), (d)(1).
[44] Code Sec. 1244(c)(1).

[45] Code Sec. 1244(c)(3).
[46] Code Sec. 1202(e).
[47] Code Sec. 1244(c)(1).

though neither corporation was held individually for more than five years.[48] Similar to Scenario A, the benefits of gain exclusion may be limited by the application of the alternative minimum tax.

Scenario C

The stock is sold on January 2, 2004 for $200,000. Bob is allowed to recognize $100,000 as ordinary loss. If the shares were not qualifying and he had no offsetting capital gains, he would only be allowed to currently deduct a $3,000 capital loss.

Scenario D

The stock becomes worthless on December 29, 2005. Bob is allowed to recognize $100,000 as ordinary loss and the remaining $200,000 is treated as capital loss. Bob may have been able to double the amount of the loss available by selling the shares for a very reduced price over a period of two years. In order to make the business saleable Bob might have invested additional funds into the company. A small investment might have allowed him to increase his loss allowance by $100,000. The availability of such a situation may vary greatly depending upon the specific business situation.

¶217 Specific Identification Method of Gain Recognition— Opportunities to Reduce Current Gain Recognition on Stock and Mutual Fund Sales

An investor may be able to minimize the recognition of gain on sales of stock and/or mutual fund sales by specifically identifying the lots that are sold. If prices are rising, an investor can choose to sell shares having the highest basis and thereby minimize gain recognition. If, however, shares sold have not been specifically identified prior to the transaction, then, in the case of stocks, use of the first-in, first-out method is required for purposes of gain/loss recognition.[49] Mutual fund shares sold, if not identified, may also qualify for averaging methods in addition to the FIFO method.

In order to use the specific identification method the agent (e.g., broker) must be informed prior to the sale to sell specific shares of stock. After the sale the agent is required to set forth a confirmation of sale of the specified lots in a written document.[50] In cases where the investor sells actual securities directly, those certificates will be the ones deemed to be sold, even if it were the intention of the investor to have securities from a different lot sold.[51]

.01 Practical Issues

As a practical matter, specific identification can work well where accurate records are maintained and the investor is willing to take the time to review them prior to generating a sales transaction. Records should include separate accounts for each stock and class within the stock category. Accounting for individual stock shares, while having some complexities, is often not as complicated as accounting for mutual fund shares.

---

[48] Additionally, the replacement stock must meet a separate six month active business requirement (Code Sec. 1045).

[49] Reg. § 1.1012-1(c)(1).
[50] Reg. § 1.1012-1(c)(3).
[51] Reg. § 1.1012-1(c)(2).

The common complexities of accounting for stock transactions include treatments of stock splits, stock dividends, and/or reorganizations. If an investor is participating in a stock dividend reinvestment plan, additional recordkeeping will be required.

Mutual funds can add further recordkeeping complexity in at least two ways. The first issue may be frequent (e.g., daily) reinvestment of dividends. An investor who makes only occasional cash contributions may find, nonetheless, that as a result of the frequent reinvestment of dividends, he has a large number of blocks of shares with various holding periods. Additionally, an investor who makes a partial sale of fund shares at a loss, may, inadvertently, find that he is subject to the wash sale provisions because of dividend reinvestments within the thirty days prior to and after the sale. These disallowed losses may create an additional level of recordkeeping. While stock reinvestment plans may also provide some complexity in this regard, it is usually on a smaller scale since dividends for most companies are issued only on a quarterly basis.

A second issue that may arise is the check-writing capability that accompanies many mutual funds. A possible option for mitigating the effect of inadvertent recognition of gains would be, where possible, to shift a portion of the fund to a second brokerage account. Funds having higher basis and/or long-term capital gain status could be used in the check writing account, while low basis and/or short-term status stock could be kept in an account without such privileges and, thereby, be protected from inadvertent recognitions of gain.

¶218 Cost Averaging Methods—Offer Simplicity and Limited Opportunities for Tax Savings, but Lack Flexibility

While specific identification of investments sold should provide maximum opportunities for controlling recognition of gains or losses, some investors may find meeting the requirements to maintain proper records to be too cumbersome and/or the requirement to properly identify securities to be too burdensome. These investors may still achieve some tax benefits, though often not as great as through the specific identification method, by employing either one of two available cost averaging methods. A significant detriment of adopting a cost averaging method, however, is that it precludes the use of the specific identification method for that fund in the future.

Initial adoption of a cost method does not technically preclude an investor from switching to an average cost method for that fund in the future. The recordkeeping burden associated with such a change, however, may be significant enough to deter some investors from making the switch. The expanded recordkeeping requirements typically arise because a change in method causes the trustee provided averaging method to become invalid. The information normally provided by the trustee is based on the assumption that *all* shares are subject to averaging. A change resulting from even just one transaction could potentially render the trustee's data invalid for current and all future years. Therefore, an investor evaluating an isolated transaction may need to weigh whether the initial tax benefits associated with a change to an averaging method outweigh current and future recordkeeping costs.

.01 Single-Category Average Cost

Cost valuations using the single category average cost method are straightforward and normally provided by mutual fund companies. These valuations are derived by dividing the total cost of shares by the number of shares held. Shares, for holding period purposes, are deemed sold on the first-in, first-out basis. In practice, tax benefits provided by using single-category average cost method will often not be as great as those available through the specific identification method. In some cases, however, particularly where there has been a rapid rise in share price, the average cost method could provide benefits that are superior to the specific cost method.

Example 13: Stephen Kingsbury is in a 35-percent marginal tax bracket and incurred the mutual fund transactions listed below. The tax consequences are shown comparing results from use of the specific identification method and from the single-category average cost method.

December 15, 2002 Bought 1,000 shares @ $10=$10,000

July 15, 2003 Bought 1,000 shares @ $25=$25,000

December 20, 2003 Sold 1,000 shares @ $35=$35,000

July 20, 2004 Sold 1,000 shares @ $35=$35,000

Specific identification method

Scenario A

Year 2003	Sell 1,000 shares bought July 15, 2003.
	Recognize short-term capital gain of $10,000.
	Taxes: $10,000 x .35=$3,500.
Year 2004	Sell 1,000 shares bought December 15, 2002.
	Recognize long-term capital gain of $25,000.
	Taxes: $25,000 x .15=$3,750.
Total taxes:	$3,500 + $3,750=$7,250.

Scenario B

Year 2003	Sell 1,000 shares bought December 15, 2002.
	Recognize long-term capital gain of $25,000.
	Taxes: 25,000 x .15=$3,750.
Year 2004	Sell 1,000 shares bought July 15, 2003.
	Recognize long-term capital gain of $10,000.
	Taxes: $10,000 x .15=$1,500.
Total taxes:	$5,250

Single-category average cost method

Year 2003	Sell 1,000 shares @ average cost=$17,500[a]
	Recognize long-term capital gain of $17,500
	Taxes: $17,500 x .15=$2,625.
Year 2004	Sell 1,000 shares @ average cost=$17,500
	Recognize long-term capital gain of $17,500
	Taxes: $17,500 x .15=$2,625.
Total taxes:	$5,250

[a] Average cost: $35,000/2,000 shares purchased=$17.50/share.

The single category method matches the lowest total tax cost available under the specific identification method, while also providing a one year $2,000 deferral of taxes. Further, this benefit is achieved without requiring complex recordkeeping and/or prior broker notification.

.02 Double-Category Average Cost Method

This method is similar to the single category average cost method, except that instead of there being one pool of shares, there are separate pools for shares having short-term and long-term holding periods. A significant disadvantage of using this system is that it requires that the broker be notified prior to sale. Many investors may find that if they are going to take the time to notify their broker, then with a little additional effort they may get a greater benefit by using the specific identification method.

Chapter 3

BOND INVESTMENTS

¶301 Municipal Bonds—In General

Municipal bonds can often provide significant tax benefits for upper income taxpayers. Generally taxpayers in the highest tax bracket have the greatest potential to benefit from municipal bonds, but this benefit may be mitigated by the application of the alternative minimum tax and state and local income taxes. The alternative minimum tax may affect taxpayers by requiring the inclusion of income generated by private activity bonds and/or by the disallowance of state and local taxes arising from out-of-state municipal bonds. State and local taxes applicable to out-of-state generated municipal bond interest may make such holdings less attractive in high rate jurisdictions.

TAX PLANNING: Prior to JGTRRA, municipal bonds were for many high tax-bracket investors the only feasible way, outside of retirement accounts, to generate fixed income that was not subject to tax at high marginal rates. The Jobs and Growth Tax Relief Reconciliation Act of 2003 created an important alternative for many of these investors by reducing the tax rates for qualifying dividends, including qualifying preferred dividends, to a maximum rate of 15 percent.

Bonds, including municipal bonds, however, have important financial attributes that, at least in some cases, will make them a more attractive investment than preferred stocks, even where there is a lower after-tax return. A primary benefit is that issuers of bonds are generally required to make regular semi-annual or annual payments. Issuers of preferred stock, alternatively, can defer payments or in some cases, where the instrument is not cumulative, even skip payments. The second benefit is that bonds have a fixed maturity date. This can be particularly important where market interest rates increase and, correspondingly, values of low-interest-paying fixed instruments decrease. A holder of a bond is assured, assuming the issuer does not go bankrupt or become insolvent, that he or she will receive the face value upon maturity. A preferred stock holder, however, has no guaranteed maturity date and may, as a result, incur capital losses upon sale that are well in excess of the $3,000 annual threshold.

The evaluation of municipal bonds for inclusion in an investor's portfolio, in addition to requiring consideration of tax factors, also requires consideration of a variety of nontax factors including the following:

1. **Bond rating.** Generally, higher grade bonds, such as AAA, generate lower yields than lower grade bonds. While most municipal bonds would be considered to be conservative investments, an increasing

number of instruments, generally referred to as high-yield bonds, are not highly secure.

TAX PLANNING: An alternative to the most secure municipal bond investments (e.g., AAA short-term insured bonds), especially for taxpayers who are not in the highest tax bracket, may be U.S. Treasury obligations. Although U.S. Treasury obligations are subject to federal taxation, they may provide the taxpayer with the following benefits:

1. No commission on sale or purchase [where transactions are conducted through *Treasury Direct* program],

2. No annual operating expenses in cases where individual bonds are purchased,

3. No need for diversification to protect against credit risk, and

4. No state and local taxes.

TAX PLANNING: While the risks of investing in high yield bonds may be significant, the rewards can be substantial. According to a study by Edward Altman, the average absolute return for high yield bonds for the twenty-two year period ending in 1999 was 12.16 percent.[1] A comparable pre-tax return for an investor in a 30 percent tax bracket would be 17.37 percent.

2. **Duration.** Generally, bonds of shorter duration generate lower yields than bonds of longer durations. An investor who, for example, purchases a twenty-year bond is at greater risk for long-term below market returns than is an investor who purchases a bond with only two years remaining to maturity. The bond yields reflect the differences in risk level.

TAX PLANNING: Generally, the difference between the yields of corporate and municipal bonds narrows as the duration of the instrument increases. Therefore, an investor who holds bonds in both taxable and tax-exempt accounts may choose to hold the short-term corporate bonds in the tax-exempt account and hold the longer-term municipal bonds in the taxable account.

PRACTICE POINTER: Research has found that bonds with maturities in excess of five years provide a less favorable balance between risk and reward than bonds with shorter maturities.[2] Advisers, therefore, should be sure their clients who might otherwise assume that municipal bonds are conservative investments, are aware that the sale of a long-term bond during a period of higher market interest rates could result in a significant loss.

---

[1] "Default and Returns on High Yield Bonds: Lessons from 1999 and Outlook for 2000-2002," by Edward I. Altman, Naeem Hukkawala, and Vellore Kshore, *Business Economics*, April 1, 2000, Volume 35, Issue 2, pp. 27-38.

[2] "Bonds as an Asset Class," by Frank Armstrong, *Morningstar.com*, November 11, 1998.

3. **Call risk.** Generally, bonds that have call provisions at low prices have higher yeilds than bonds that have either high call provisions or no call provisions.

PRACTICE POINTER: Selection of an acceptable call provision may depend upon the investor's purpose for holding the bond. If an investor is planning to rely on fixed interest payments for a long period of time (e.g., some retired individuals) then a relatively low call price may be unacceptable. If, however, the investor does not necessarily have a long-time horizon for holding the investment, then a relatively low call price may be acceptable, since the amount received for payment of a call premium will normally be taxed at reduced capital gains rates.

4. **Individual bonds or funds.** Generally, diversification is more difficult to achieve through individual bonds than with funds. Purchases and sales of individual bonds may also require the paying of commissions. Holders of lightly traded individual bonds may also have difficulty liquidating them prior to maturity or may have to incur a high bid-ask spread.[3] Operating expenses may be a particularly important consideration for short-term and/or high-grade funds, since the pre-expense return may be relatively small.

PRACTICE POINTER: Individuals who plan on holding bonds to maturity may benefit by purchasing lightly traded bonds, where there is a large bid-ask spread.

PRACTICE POINTER: An alternative to short-term high-grade municipal bond funds may be treasury obligations purchased through *Treasury Direct*. If, for example, a short-term municipal bond fund is yielding 4 percent before expenses and operating expenses are 0.8 percent, then the fund's expenses are reducing return by 20 percent.

Alternatively, purchasing high-yield bonds through a fund may be beneficial because:

a. There is not an individual high yield treasury security that provides an offset to the loss of diversification, and

b. The operating expenses for a high-yield fund will normally account for a smaller percentage of the total pre-expense return.

5. **Purchase at par, discount, or premium.** Theoretically, the net yield for bonds purchased at par, discount, or premium should be the same but, in practice, does not always occur.

---

[3] The vast number of small issues may make them difficult to sell. Seventy-one percent of municipal bond issuers have less than $10 million in bonds outstanding, per "Investments: Bonds: Tax Aspects of Municipal Bonds. There's More to Municipal Bonds than Tax-Free Interest," by Van E. Johnson and Linda M. Johnson, *Journal of Accountancy*, April 1996, pp. 51-55.

PRACTICE POINTER: Bonds purchased at a premium may provide a return yielding an additional ten basis points. Investors, apparently, are somewhat averse to purchasing bonds with a "premium" price.[4]

Although interest earned from municipal bonds is tax-exempt, income attributable to a discount in purchase price is subject to tax. If the discount is less than 1/4 of 1 percent of the stated redemption price, the income attributable to the discount will be capital gain. If the discount is greater than that amount, the income attributable to the discount is taxable as ordinary income.

Example 1: Karen Johnson purchases an 8 percent, $100,000 municipal bond maturing in five years for $97,000. Since the amount of the discount is more than $1,250 [$100,000 x .0025 x 5 years], Karen would recognize $3,000 in ordinary income upon maturity. If the amount of the discount had been less than $1,250, the gain recognized upon maturity would be taxable as capital gain. In either case the $8,000/year of interest income would be tax-exempt.

TAX PLANNING: Taxpayers currently in high tax brackets may benefit by purchasing discounted municipal bonds that are scheduled to mature at a time when they expect to be in a lower bracket (e.g., after retirement). A taxpayer, for example, who seeks fixed income, may benefit by receiving annual interest income payments that, from other sources (e.g., bank interest) would be subject to a 35 percent tax bracket. After retirement, the taxpayer may benefit by paying taxes at a lower marginal rate (e.g., 25 percent) on the difference between the bond's purchase and redemption prices. If the bond were to be called early, the taxpayer would only be subject to ordinary income on the ratable increase in bond value. Any excess would be taxable at capital gains rates.

6. **Insured or non-insured bonds.** Generally, the yield for insured bonds is lower than for non-insured bonds. Insured municipal bonds, however, that are normally insured by private insurance companies, still do not have the same level of security as directly held U.S. Treasury obligations.

7. **Evaluation of yield and net asset value.** Evaluation of a fund's yield may be misleading because a fund manager may purchase bonds of longer duration or greater risk in order to initially maintain a fund's yield. Additionally, if absolute investment returns remain the same, but net asset values decline (e.g., long-term bond is held during time of rising interest rates), then the yield will be shown to *increase* (return is a higher percentage of a shrunken asset base), a result that could potentially mislead some potential investors.

PRACTICE POINTER: In evaluating the performance of a bond fund, the total return should be considered: yield plus capital appreciation.

---

[4] Reported in "Finding the Value of Municipal Bonds," by George Van Dyke, *Business Credit*, June 1999, Vol. 101, Issue 6, pp. 34-35.

8. **Comparability with corporate and/or U.S. government obligations.** Generally, strict comparison may be difficult. It may be difficult to compare, for example, a lower grade corporate bond with a U.S. treasury obligation. Similarly, it may be difficult to compare a municipal bond with a business in a specialized industry (e.g., telecommunications) where long-term viability is significantly affected by demand for a specialized service.

¶302 Marginal Federal, State and Local Tax Rates May Affect Choice of Municipal Bonds

Municipal bonds, in general, provide an increasing benefit as an individual's marginal tax bracket rises. The tax benefit is greatest, relative to corporate bonds, for individuals who live in high tax jurisdictions and purchase bonds that are nontaxable in their own state. Interestingly, though, the incremental benefit of investing in in-state bonds, as opposed to out-of-state bonds, is greater for taxpayers in low federal tax brackets than for individuals in high federal tax brackets. Therefore, individuals in the highest federal tax bracket may have the greatest incentive to purchase out-of-state bonds, since they can achieve the benefits of diversification at the lowest incremental cost.

The following example illustrates the effect of state and local taxes for a variety of tax rate conditions. In general, most states tax out-of-state municipal bond interest while exempting income generated from their own jurisdiction.[5]

Example 2: The following example shows required equivalent municipal bond rates for an individual earning 10 percent per year in corporate bond interest.

Taxpayer A

Federal tax bracket—35%

State and local tax bracket—7.5%

Net tax rate (assuming state and local taxes deductible)—39.875%

Required municipal bond interest rate (nontaxable for state)—6.0125%

Required municipal bond interest rate (taxable for state)[6]—6.3206%[7]

Taxpayer B

Federal tax bracket —35%

State and local tax bracket—0%

Net tax rate—35%

Required municipal bond interest rate (nontaxable for state)—6.5%

Required municipal bond interest rate (taxable for state)—6.5%

---

[5] Taxes on out-of-state municipal bond interest are *not*, however, imposed by Indiana, Utah, and the District of Columbia. Alternatively, the following states tax both in-state and out-of-state municipal bond interest: Illinois, Iowa, Kansas, Oklahoma, and Wisconsin.

[6] Effective state tax rate: state tax rate 7.5% - federal tax benefit for deducting state taxes (7.5% x .35) = 4.875%.

[7] Out-of-state municipal bond interest 6.3206% - (6.3206 x effective state rate .04875) = 6.0125% [equivalent in-state bond rate].

Taxpayer C
Federal tax bracket—25%
State and local tax bracket—7.5%
Net tax rate—30.625%
Required municipal bond interest rate (nontaxable for state)—6.9375%
Required municipal bond interest rate (taxable for state)[8]—7.3510%

Taxpayer D
Federal tax bracket —15%
State and local tax bracket—7.5%
Net tax rate (assuming state and local taxes deductible)—21.375%
Required municipal bond interest rate (nontaxable for state)—7.8625%
Required municipal bond interest rate (taxable for state)[9] —8.3979%

Taxpayer E
Federal tax bracket —15%
State and local tax bracket—0%
Net tax rate (assuming state and local taxes deductible)—15%
Required municipal bond interest rate (nontaxable for state)—8.5%
Required municipal bond interest rate (taxable for state)—8.5%

The example illustrates, in general :

1. Taxpayers residing in jurisdictions with high state and local tax rates receive greater benefits from municipal bonds than individuals residing in jurisdictions with no or low state and local tax rates. The benefit is illustrated, in two comparisons: *Taxpayers A* vs. *B* and *Taxpayers D* vs. *E*.

2. Taxpayers in high federal tax brackets, residing in high state and local tax jurisdictions, do *not* receive the greatest benefit from holding in-state municipal bonds (as opposed to out-of-state bonds). Rather, because state and local taxes are deductible on a federal tax return, individuals in the lowest marginal federal tax bracket receive the greatest incremental benefit from holding a concentrated portfolio of in-state bonds. *Taxpayer A*, for example, receives less incremental benefit from holding in-state bonds than *Taxpayer C*. *Taxpayer D*, who because of his low federal tax rate would not be a good candidate for municipal bonds, theoretically receives the greatest incremental benefit from holding in-state bonds.

PRACTICE POINTER: Despite marketing campaigns touting the benefits of in-state municipal bonds and/or funds to the highest marginal income

---

[8] Effective state tax rate: 7.5% - (7.5% x .25) = 5.625%.

[9] Effective state tax rate: 7.5% - (7.5% x .15) = 6.375%.

taxpayers, such taxpayers may actually be able to enjoy the benefits of diversification at the lowest marginal cost.

3. Individuals residing in no or low tax jurisdictions receive no or only minimal incremental benefit from holding only in-state bonds. Therefore, individuals from no-tax jurisdictions should only be holding diversified municipal bond portfolios.

4. Taxpayers, in low tax brackets generally receive little total benefit from municipal bonds, even if their state and local tax rate is high. A potential secure alternative for *Taxpayer E,* who resides in a high tax jurisdiction, could be to invest in U.S. Treasury obligations.

¶303 High-Yield Municipal Bond Risk May Be Diffused through Fund Investments

An investor who directly holds high-yield municipal bonds may be putting himself at greater than average risk of incurring losses beyond the $3,000 annual capital loss allowance. A 1999 study by Fitch, a bond-rating firm in New York, found, for example, that the default rate for non-rated and below investment grade municipal bonds was between 3 percent and 4 percent. The rate for industrial development bonds was even higher, approximately 15 percent.[10] The risk for bondholders of incurring nondeductible capital losses is illustrated by the following example.

Example 3: Jane Renault directly holds five $50,000 high yield bonds. Four of the bonds generate $6,000 each (12 percent annual return) for a total of $24,000. The other bond pays no interest and becomes worthless during the year. Assuming there are no other capital losses, only $3,000 can be deducted during the year and $47,000 must be carried forward. The $24,000 in interest income provides no offset to the capital loss.

If, alternatively, Jane is holding investments with significant built-in capital gains, then the potential inability to claim capital losses may not be an issue. Still, even for those taxpayers for whom the capital loss allowance is not an issue, concern with potential *economic* losses may be sufficient to lead them to purchase bonds through a fund, in order to diffuse the risk of default.

PRACTICE POINTER: When evaluating risk of municipal bonds, investors should weigh the relative risk of different sectors. A study found, for example, that the default rate for water and sewer bonds issued between 1979 and 1986 was 0.4 percent, while the default rate for health care bonds was 2.62 percent.[11]

PRACTICE POINTER: Attempts to identify specific high yield bond investments may carry special risks not found in the equities market.

---

[10] As reported in "Stock-Like Risk is 'Ugly Secret' in Usually Safe Muni Market," by Karen Damato, *The Wall Street Journal Interactive Edition,* March 28, 2001.

[11] "Fitch's Report on Defaults Could Affect Riskier Sectors Insurability," by Jennifer Karchmer, *Bond Buyer,* September 20, 1999, Vol. 329, Issue 30729, pp. 2-8.

Whereas publicly held companies generally issue quarterly financial information with the SEC, municipal bond issuers often provide information on an annual basis. Further, since the SEC is prohibited from requiring specific disclosures of municipal bond issuers, the information released may be incomplete or even misleading.

PRACTICE POINTER: Holding a portfolio containing both high quality and high yield bonds may provide enhanced diversification benefits. Correlations between high yield and high quality bonds tend to be lower than that of different sectors of the stock market.[12] Many more opportunities are currently available to invest in high yield bonds than in the recent past.

¶304 Alternative Minimum Tax Considerations—Additional Uncertainty Following Passage of EGTRRA & JGTRRA

Individuals evaluating what types of municipal bonds, if any, to include in their portfolio should consider both existing and future applications of the AMT provisions. The two primary direct effects of the alternative minimum tax, currently in effect are:

1. The inclusion of interest income earned from private activity bonds, and

2. Disallowance of state and local income taxes.

The extent of future applications may, however, be difficult to gage. The alternative minimum tax exclusion for individuals was increased, first under the Economic Growth and Tax Relief Act of 2001, and then again under the Jobs Growth and Tax Relief Reconciliation Act of 2003 but, in both cases, only on a temporary basis. The exemption for married couples filing joint returns, for example, was increased from $45,000 to $49,000 and then to $58,000 under EGTRRA and JGTRRA, respectively. The increased exemption amounts, however, are scheduled to revert back to $45,000 for tax years beginning after 2004.[13] Whether or not that provision will expire, be modified, or made permanent is a political decision for which planners do not yet have an answer.

TAX PLANNING: Individuals who, except for the AMT disallowance of state and local taxes, would otherwise invest in a diverse portfolio of municipal bonds may wish to consider U.S. savings obligations as an alternative, since such investments are:

1. Not subject to state and local taxation,

2. Provide even higher credit protection than that offered by high-grade municipal bonds, and

3. In the case of savings bonds, offer opportunities for tax deferral, although not federal tax-exclusion.

---

[12] According to T. Rowe Price Vice President Steven Norwitz, as reported in "Bond Market Diversification is an option for 'Chickens' by Jonathan Clements, *The Wall Street Journal*, July 24, 2001.

[13] Further, the number of individuals subject to the AMT is expected to drastically increase over the next decade. According to a Dept. of Treasury analysis, by the year 2010, 32 percent of taxpayers with incomes between $50,000 and $75,000 and four personal exemptions are expected to be subject to the AMT, per Dept. of Treasury, Office of Tax Analysis Working Paper 87, June 2000.

Similarly, investors who currently qualify for the increased AMT exclusion, but would not after 2004, may consider investing only in short-term municipal bonds until that time. While, theoretically, an investor could invest in any duration municipal bond and sell prior to expiration of the expanded AMT provisions, it may be more likely that the value of longer-term funds may fall, in the event that the expanded exclusion amount is not renewed.

¶305 Private Activity Bonds Create Both Risks and Opportunities

Interest from specified private activity bonds issued after August 7, 1986 is considered a tax preference item and, therefore, must be added back to taxable income for purposes of computing alternative minimum taxable income. Taxpayers who believe they may become subject to the AMT should, therefore, in most cases avoid holding them as investments. Also, investors who are not comfortable with the speculative nature of their future tax treatment may also wish to avoid them. While under EGTRRA more taxpayers are expected to become subject to the AMT, a number of political efforts have been made to reduce or eliminate its application.

TAX PLANNING: Investors who are highly certain that they will not be subject to the AMT may purchase private activity bonds and potentially obtain higher returns for municipal bond interest, in addition to the amount received for the higher credit risk, because the market of potential purchasers of private activity bonds is smaller than that for private activity bonds. Alternatively, investors who purchase private activity bonds and unexpectedly find themselves subject to the AMT could be left with two unsatisfactory choices:

1. Hold the bonds and recognize private activity bond interest income, or

2. Sell the bond and incur nondeductible current losses (beyond the $3,000 annual capital loss limitation).

PRACTICE POINTER: The uncertain future of the alternative minimum tax should be a consideration for taxpayers who believe they may need to liquidate their bonds prior to redemption. If, in fact, more taxpayers become subject to the AMT, the number of potential buyers for private activity bonds may be further reduced, increasing the probability that the bond may lose value. Alternatively, if the AMT is repealed, values of existing private activity bonds may increase, reflecting the larger market of buyers.

¶306 Ultra-Short Bond Funds May Provide a Viable Alternative to Short-Term Municipal Bond Funds

Investors who are willing to accept a modest amount of risk may find ultra-short corporate bond funds to be a viable alternative to short-term municipal bond funds. The pre-tax spread between municipal and corporate obligations is often greatest for bonds of short-term duration. Therefore, oftentimes, only taxpayers in the highest tax brackets stand to receive an after-tax benefit from holding short-term municipal bond obligations.

The benefit of investing in an ultra-short bond fund is to receive a return that is nearly comparable to that generated by short-term bond funds, while being subject to a significantly lower level of risk. According to a study by Morningstar, the average annual rate of return for a short-term bond fund for the three-year period ending July 16, 2001 was 5.89 percent, while the average annual return for ultra-short bond funds was 5.45 percent. The risk, however, for holding the average ultra-short fund, however, was less than half of that of the short-term bond fund.[14]

> **PRACTICE POINTER:** If absolute or virtually absolute credit security is required, then U.S. Treasury obligations should be purchased. If, however, the taxpayer is willing to assume a minimal level of risk, then it may make sense to compare the after-tax returns of municipal bond funds with ultra-short bond funds. Some ultra-short funds may provide state and local tax benefits by holding U.S. treasury obligations. The holding of these obligations further provides the benefit of reducing credit risk within the fund.

¶307 Short-Term Treasury Investments May Provide a Viable Alternative to Tax-Exempt or Taxable Money Market Funds

Taxpayers who seek safe short-term investments often choose money market investments. Investors may, however, receive greater security and/or higher after-tax returns by investing in short-term Treasury obligations. While short-term Treasury securities do not provide the immediate liquidity of money market funds, opportunities to access funds may be sufficient to make short-term Treasury securities a viable option to money market accounts.

Opportunities to invest in short-term Treasury securities now include 4-week Treasuries (actually reopenings of existing 13 and 26 week bills). These bills, currently are not sold through the *Treasury Direct*, a program that allows investors to purchase securities directly from the Treasury department without commission, but can be used for reinvestment in their program for 13 or 26 week bills.

> **PRACTICE POINTER:** An evaluation of a money market fund's performance should include consideration of the relative safety of its portfolio. Some taxable money market funds, for example, may achieve higher returns by investing heavily in commercial paper, an investment that may be significantly more risky than Treasuries or high-grade municipal bonds. Tax-exempt money market funds may boost returns by including higher percentages of low-grade bonds.

> **TAX PLANNING:** Short-term Treasuries (4, 13, and 26 week durations) provide opportunities, not available with money market funds, to defer

---

[14] "Our Favorite Ultrashort Bond Funds," by Scott Berry, *Morningstar.com*, July 19, 2001.

income until the next year. Income on these short-term securities is not recognized until the earlier of when the bond matures or is sold.

¶308 Inflation Adjusted U.S. Savings Bonds (I-Bonds) May Provide Opportunities to Hedge Inflation While Deferring or, in Some Cases, Excluding Income

I-bonds, as do EE savings bonds, provide for a deferral of income until redemption,[15] but unlike EE bonds also provide a hedge against inflation that should be significantly more reliable than more traditional inflation-hedging vehicles, such as real estate and precious metals. The tax deferral feature of I-bonds may, in some cases, make them more advantageous than Treasury inflation-indexed securities (TIPS),[16] the original inflation-adjusted security offered by the Treasury Department, even though TIPS normally will provide a higher pre-tax return. Also, in some cases, where the proceeds of I-bonds are used for qualifying educational expenses, income may be excluded.

The earnings rate of I-bonds is composed of two parts, a fixed rate of interest and a variable inflation adjusted rate. The fixed rate of interest remains in effect for the life of the bond, while the variable rate is adjusted semiannually based on changes in the Consumer Price Index for all Urban Consumers (CPI-U). In the unlikely event of deflation, in which case the CPI-U would decline, the negative return would reduce the fixed portion of interest income for the current year. In no case, however, would there be a reduction in redemption value of the bond.[17]

.01 Potential Detriments and Limitations of I-Bond Investing

Investing in I-bonds, while shielding the investor from credit risk, does provide some economic risks. Probably, the most significant risk of holding I-bonds is that if the inflation rate is low, the rate of return may be lower than what might have been available from instruments offering fixed rates of return. Investors interested in maintaining a diversified portfolio, therefore, will likely choose to hold both inflation-adjusted and fixed instruments. The second risk is that if an investor is required to redeem the bonds prior to holding them for five years, he or she will be subject to a three months earnings penalty.

One limitation of investing in I-bonds is that only $30,000 per individual may be purchased each year. These bonds, however, may also be purchased for children. A family of four, therefore, could purchase $120,000 worth of I-bonds per year. Another limitation, similar to EE Savings Bonds, is that bonds issued to children are not eligible for the exclusion for bonds used for higher education. Even, however, where the bonds are held by parents or other adults, the relatively low level of income allowed to benefit from the exclusion (e.g., phaseout for modified adjusted gross income between $86,400 and $116,400 for

---

[15] Taxes cannot be deferred for more than 30 years.

[16] In practice, TIPS serves as an acronym for Treasury Inflation Protection-Securities, the term that is commonly used to refer to the Treasury's inflation-indexed securities.

[17] A good source of basic information about I-bonds can be obtained at www.savingsbonds.gov/sav/sbinvest.htm.

joint filers in the year 2002),[18] may preclude many taxpayers from the opportunity to exclude interest income.

.02 Deferring Income to Take Advantage of Lower Marginal Tax Brackets

Individuals who anticipate that they or their children will be in a lower tax bracket in the future may particularly benefit from the tax deferral feature of I-bonds. The new 10 percent bracket may further enhance the attractiveness of I-bonds as a tax deferral vehicle.

> **Example 4:** Bob and Barbara Benson purchase $15,000 of I-bonds for their daughter, Bernice, who is age 9. Since the total gift is under $22,000,[19] no gift tax is due on the return. The bonds are assumed to earn 6 percent per year. The daughter is in the 10 percent tax bracket and is assumed to have no other income. After five years, at age 14, the bond is redeemed at its value of $20,070. After payment of $507 in taxes, the remaining $19,563 is reinvested for another five years and then redeemed, at which point the child is age 19. The taxpayer is left with a net amount of $25,518, following payment of $662 in taxes. As a result of the intermediate redemption followed by reinvestment the taxpayer is able to benefit by having all income recognized at the 10 percent rate. Further, the Bensons may benefit by not wasting a standard deduction or state and local tax exemptions.

.03 I-Bonds for Individuals Contemplating Early Retirement

Individuals who are contemplating retirement prior to age 59 1/2 may find I-bonds to be particularly effective for deferring income and providing flexibility to recognize only the amount of income needed in the current year. The order in which I-bonds are redeemed can also play an important role in minimizing taxes.

> **Example 5:** Nera Allen, age 40, is contemplating early retirement at age 50. She purchases $30,000/year of I-bonds for ten years to help fund her retirement.

> At age 50, assuming Nera is attempting to minimize taxes, she should redeem first the bonds she purchased at age 45, since those are the ones with the shortest time periods that can be redeemed without being subject to a penalty for a loss of interest for bonds held less than five years. At age 51, she should redeem the bonds purchased at age 46 and continue this pattern of redeeming bonds held for the minimum five-year pattern until she redeems the bonds purchased at age 49. The following years she should redeem the bonds purchased at age 44, followed by the bonds purchased at ages 43, 42, 41, and 40, as a means of maximizing the amount of the tax deferral period.

I-bonds can also provide excellent tax deferrals for individuals such as professional athletes who are likely to retire prior to age 59 1/2 and see a decline in their marginal tax brackets. Such individuals can draw on these funds without

---

[18] Rev. Proc. 2001-59.

[19] The gift tax annual exclusion in 2002 is $11,000 per individual (Rev. Proc. 2001-59, 2001-52 IRB 1).

being subject to penalties for drawing on funds from retirement accounts prior to the age 59 1/2 age, or, in some cases, the age 55 threshold.

¶309 Treasury Inflation-Protected Securities (TIPS) Provide Inflation Hedging Benefits but Require Recognition of Non-cash Income

Treasury Inflation Protected Securities generally provide the opportunity to receive a higher inflation adjusted return than that offered by I-bonds, but have requirements for income recognition that may make them less desirable for taxable accounts. Whereas I-bonds allow for deferral of income until the bond is redeemed, TIPS require recognition of accrued, but undistributed, increases in the value of the instrument.

TIPS and I-bonds vary in a variety of ways. First, while all income for I-bonds is accrued until redemption, TIPS pay out a fixed percentage of income semi-annually based on an inflation-adjusted increase in principal. The fixed percentage rate of interest is determined at auction and is normally somewhat higher than that offered for I-bonds. The accrued portion, as is the case with I-bonds is determined based on the Consumer Price Index for all Urban Consumers (CPI-U).

TAX PLANNING: The requirement that taxpayers must recognize accrued but undistributed taxable income is probably the primary factor that makes TIPS investments, for some investors, less desirable then I-bonds. TIPS, however, because of their normally higher interest rates than I-bonds, are likely to be the more optimal choice for tax-deferred or tax-exempt accounts. Similarly, taxpayers in lower tax brackets may benefit less from the tax deferral feature of I-bonds and find that the TIPS investment yields a higher after-tax return. This may be particularly true for taxpayers who are in the new 10 percent tax bracket.

TAX PLANNING: TIPS may be attractive investments for minors who might otherwise be subject to the "kiddie tax," but have less than $750 in taxable income. A ten year TIPS might initially be purchased and held until the income generated reaches thresholds of either taxability (e.g. standard deduction) or absorption of the 10 percent tax bracket. The securities could be sold prior to maturity date through the U.S. Treasury's *Sell Direct* program, a component of its *Treasury Direct* program. Under this program the Treasury, for a $34 fee, obtains quotes from different brokers and sells the securities at the best price offered for them.[20] Following the sale, if an inflation-adjusted investment is still desired, then the purchase of an I-bond may be an optimal choice. Purchase of an I-bond will allow deferral of income recognition for a period of an additional thirty years.

Other distinctions between I-bonds and TIPS include:

---

[20] More information about this program can be found at *www.publicdebt.treas.gov/sec/secselld.htm.*

1. TIPS are issued for periods of fixed duration: currently being issued only in ten-year terms. I-bonds can be redeemed any time after five years without penalty and held without recognition of income for a period of up to 30 years.

2. TIPS can be purchased through the Treasury Direct program in amounts up to $5 million for Treasury auctions. I-bond purchases are limited to $30,000/individual per year.

¶310 Convertible Bonds Can Achieve a Tax-Deferred Conversion from Debt to Equity, while also Generating Low Volatility

Convertible bonds provide a tax-deferred opportunity to shift from a debt to an equity instrument. Whereas the sale of a bond followed by purchase of stock in the same company would require capital gain recognition on any appreciation in the value of the bond, no such recognition is required when a convertible bond is converted into stock.[21]

Convertible bonds have also provided the benefit, at least over the ten-year period ending December 31, 2000 of lower volatility than most stocks and bonds, while generating respectable returns. Hedge Fund Research tracked 63 convertible bond funds and found that they generated an average annual return of 11.8 percent with an average standard deviation of only 3.5 percent. The performance compared favorably with the S&P 500 (average return of 13.8 percent and standard deviation of 13.9 percent) and the Lehman Brothers Government/Corporate Bond Index (average return of 9.7 percent and standard deviation of 5 percent).[22]

> **PRACTICE POINTER:** Convertible bond funds also provide an excellent means of increasing diversification within a portfolio. During the ten year period ended December 31, 2000, the 63 convertible bond funds tracked had a correlation to the Lehman Government/Corporate Bond Index of only 19 percent and to the S&P 500 of 38 percent.[23] In order to maintain low correlations, investors should avoid "deep in the money" convertibles bonds. Such bonds have appreciated to the point that their price movement follows closely that of the issuer's stock.

> **PRACTICE POINTER:** Funds may provide the most cost-effective opportunities to invest in convertible bonds. The convertible bond market is dominated largely by institutions, which may make it difficult for individuals to get a good price on purchases.[24]

---

[21] Rev. Rul. 72-265.

[22] "Reveling in Volatility," by Laurie Kaplan Singh, *Institutional Investor*, June 2001, Vol. 35, Issue 6, pp. 141-143.

[23] *Ibid.*

[24] "Bonds: Time to Cruise for Convertibles?" by Toddi Gutner, *Business Week*, December 1, 1997, page 180.

¶311 Market Discount Bonds Provide Opportunities to Partially Defer Income Recognition

Bonds purchased at a market discount provide an opportunity to partially defer recognition of income until they are sold or redeemed. Whereas bonds issued at original discount require the holder to recognize the daily portion of OID for each day the instrument is held, holders of market discount bonds can defer recognition of income from the market discount portion until the date of sale.[25] The gain that is ultimately recognized from income attributable to market discount, however, is treated as ordinary income.

> **TAX PLANNING:** Market discount bonds may provide good opportunities to achieve a partial deferral of income until an individual is in a lower tax bracket. The availability of higher quality market discount bonds may, however, often depend upon the current state of the economy and inflation. Bonds, for example, that were issued when prevailing rates were low, may lose value in cases where there is a sudden increase in inflation and interest rates rise. Although the value of the bond has declined, the credit worthiness of the company may be unchanged. Alternatively, under a condition of declining interest rates, the only market discount bonds available may be those whose credit worthiness has declined.

.01 Market-Discount Ginnie Maes May Provide Deferral Opportunities for Children and/or Retirement Funding

Investments in discounted Ginnie Maes may offer benefits for individuals who can reasonably anticipate a time when they will be in a lower tax bracket. This benefit may arise because the built-in gain[26] is not recognized until the maturity date, similar to the general treatment for market-discount bonds, or until the face amount of the securities is prepaid. A further benefit is that part of the monthly payments constitutes a tax-free return of capital. If the taxpayer is willing to hold the securities until maturity, the purchaser can be guaranteed favorable treatment either through recognition of taxable income at a lower marginal tax rate or at a capital gain in the event of prepayment.

> **Example 6:** Sam and Sarah Smith in 2003 purchase $25,000, maturity value of Ginnie Maes, due date of 2008, at a cost of $20,000 for their 10 year old son, Shawn. The securities pay 6 percent of their face, generating $1,500/year in income. Since the income generated does not exceed $1,500, none of the income is subject to the "kiddie tax." If the investment is not prepaid and matures in 2008, Shawn will be required to recognize the income at ordinary rates, but it will be at his own rate of taxable income, rather than his parents. This income would likely be taxed at 10 percent or 15 percent.

---

[25] A taxpayer may also elect to report market discount income on a current basis (Code Sec. 1278(b)). The election, however, would apply to all market discount bonds acquired in that year and all future years. Further, that election can only be revoked by consent of the IRS.

[26] Assuming held-to-maturity.

If alternatively, the securities were prepaid prior to Shawn turning age 14, Shawn would be required to recognize the ratable portion of the increase at his parent's ordinary income rates. Any amount above the ratable portion, however, would be subject to capital gains rates.

TAX PLANNING: Since Ginnie Mae investments are subject to state and local income taxes, they generally must offer an increased rate of return to compensate investors for that cost. Taxpayers who live in states that have no or low income taxes, therefore, may benefit by receiving higher income while incurring no or only minimal tax liability.

Chapter 4

REAL ESTATE

¶401 Real Estate Investment Trusts (REITs) Provide Opportunities for Portfolio Diversification with Modest Tax Benefits

REITs provide individual investors with the opportunity to invest in large-scale commercial real estate enterprises with, in most cases, greater liquidity than that afforded by traditional limited real estate partnerships. An important attribute of REITs is that they can reduce risk within a portfolio by providing an increase in diversification. A recent study, discussed in ¶401.03, found a relatively low correlation between REITs and both large and small stocks, as well as with long-term bonds.[1]

REITs typically generate ordinary taxable income through annual or more frequent distributions but, nonetheless, may provide some tax benefits through distributions that are:

1. Treated as returns of capital, and/or

2. Treated as capital gains.

.01 Structure and Operation of REITs

Entities may qualify for REIT status and avoid the double taxation status of C Corporations by fulfilling a number of requirements, including the following:[2]

- Generate at least 75 percent of income from real estate,

- Generate at least 95 percent of income from real estate, interest, dividends, and gains from sale of stock and securities,

- Maintain at least 100 shareholders,

- Maintain broad-based ownership,

- Limit securities holdings of any single issuer, and

- Pay dividends of at least 90 percent of ordinary and foreclosure income.

Undistributed income of a REIT, if any, is subject to tax at ordinary corporate rates. REITs may, however, pass through capital gains to their shareholders as capital gains dividends.

---

[1] "REITs' Low Correlation to Other Stocks and Bonds is Key Factor for Portfolio Diversification," News release of National Association of Real Estate Investment Trusts, May 29, 2001, contains findings from analysis prepared by Ibbotson Associates.

[2] Code Secs. 856 and 857 contain the full set of requirements.

.02 Tax Benefits of REITs

REITs may be able to distribute some payments to shareholders as returns of capital, rather than as taxable dividends, because of the entity's depreciation deduction.

> **Example 1:** Ready REIT has zero earnings and profits as of the beginning of the year. During the year the REIT generates $600,000 in ordinary taxable income, including a $100,000 reduction for depreciation, even though the property has actually increased in value during the year. Ready REIT, with adequate cash flow, distributes $700,000 to its shareholders. Only $600,000 is subject to tax, since the remaining $100,000 represents a return of capital.

Income from the sale of appreciated real estate property may generate income that is subject to preferred capital gains rates (e.g., 18 percent or 20 percent). If the property has been acquired after 1986, the property will not be subject to the 25 percent rate for depreciation recapture.[3]

> **Example 2:** Renata REIT sells a commercial building in 2007 for $1,000,000. The building had originally been purchased in 2001 for $800,000. At the time of the sale, $100,000 in depreciation had been claimed and the entity's basis in the building is $700,000. Renata will pass through to the shareholders $300,000 in income subject to a maximum rate of 18 percent (capital gain rate for property held more than five years).

A potential disadvantage of REITs, similar to other public corporations, is that they are prohibited from passing losses through to their shareholders. Since holdings in any one entity are normally limited to five percent or less, however, even holders in an equivalent partnership would normally not be eligible to claim such losses.[4]

> **PRACTICE POINTER:** A practical benefit for some shareholders of investing in real estate through REITS, rather than through limited partnerships, is that the shareholder is not required to file tax returns in nonresident states for out-of-state properties. Similarly, it is not necessary for shareholders to keep track of basis and passive loss limitations for individual activities within a real estate investment. This benefit may be particularly helpful to a number of individuals who hold modest percentages of real estate within their portfolio, primarily for purposes of increasing diversification within their portfolio. If, for example a client has a $500,000 portfolio and desires to hold 5% in real estate, only $25,000 will be invested in such properties. If he is forced to sustain additional costs for preparation of out-of-state tax returns and complex record-keeping such investment may not be cost effective.

---

[3] Recapture tax rates may apply to properties purchased prior to 1987, where depreciation had been claimed using an accelerated method.

[4] Active participants who hold 10 percent or more of a property and meet certain income requirements may qualify for current deductions of rental losses.

.03 REITs May Provide Portfolio Diversification and Thereby Reduce Risk

REITs may provide excellent opportunities to increase diversification and thereby reduce risk within a portfolio. A study conducted by Ibbotson Associates found relatively low and decreasing levels of correlation between REITS and both large and small stocks. Correlation levels between REITs and bonds have been and remain low. In the 1980s, for example, the correlation between small stocks[5] and REITs was 74 percent, whereas for the period 1993-2000 the correlation rate was only 26 percent. Similarly, the correlation between REITs and large stocks[6] for the 1980s was 65 percent and for the period 1993-2000 was 25 percent. The rate for bonds during the 1980s was 17 percent and for the period 1993-2000 was 16 percent. The low correlations may provide increased protection against simultaneously incurring poor performance through all components of a portfolio.

While many investors may choose to include investments in REITs as a means of diversifying their portfolio, many may wish to limit their holdings in this sector because of the following potential inherent risks:

- Market risk—potential for prolonged downturns in real estate market,
- Interest rate risk—interest rate increases may hurt valuations,
- Environmental liability risk—potential liability for hazardous materials (e.g., asbestos), and
- Uninsured damage.

The compound annual return for REITs during the period 1981- 2000 was 12.43 percent, whereas the compound annual rate for U.S. small stocks was 13.33 percent and for the S&P 500 was 15.68 percent.

    TAX PLANNING: Where the space in tax-deferred retirement accounts is not sufficient to hold both REITs and common stocks within a tax-deferred retirement account, placement of the REIT within the tax-deferred account may be advantageous because

1. The preponderance of dividends from REITs do not qualify for tax-advantaged dividend rates (e.g., 15 percent),
2. REITs generally pay higher dividends than do common stocks, and
3. Distributions from the retirement account would generally not result in dividends losing tax-advantaged status, as would be the case with common stocks.

In many cases it may be necessary to prepare calculations to determine which combination would be expected to yield the best after-tax return.

---

[5] Ibbotson U.S. Small Stock Series.   [6] S&P 500 Index.

¶402 "Actively" Managed Real Estate May Provide Opportunities for Current Ordinary Loss Deductions and Capital Gain Recognition

Individuals with adjusted gross income under $150,000 who "actively participate" in rental real estate enterprises may be able to claim some losses that would otherwise be disallowed by application of the passive loss rules. In general, individuals whose adjusted gross income is $100,000 or less may deduct the full amount of their qualifying losses from rental properties to a maximum of $25,000. Individuals who have higher AGI will have their potential loss allowance reduced by 50 percent of the amount by which their AGI exceeds $100,000. The exact amount allowed may vary depending upon adjustments for IRA deductions, Social Security benefits, interest deductions, qualified tuition, and losses from passive activities.[7]

Qualification for active participation requires that the taxpayer own 10 percent or more in value of the property and that she participates in either making or arranging of management decisions in a significant and bona fide sense.

> **Example 3:** Bert and Brenda Miller have adjusted gross income of $130,000 and incur $12,000 in losses from actively managed real estate. Their current allowable loss is determined as follows:
>
> | | | |
> |---|---:|---:|
> | Maximum allowable loss before threshold reduction | | $25,000 |
> | Adjusted gross income | $130,000 | |
> | Threshold amount – | $100,000 | |
> | | $ 30,000 | |
> | Disallowance rate | x .50 | |
> | Maximum allowable after threshold reduction | | 15,000 |
> | Bert and Brenda's loss is limited to $10,000. | | $10,000 |

.01 JGTRRA Creates Window to Benefit from 50 Percent Bonus Depreciation

JGTRRA increased the allowance for additional first-year depreciation from 30 percent to 50 percent for assets that are acquired after May 3, 2005 and placed in service before January 1, 2005.[8] The allowance is generally applicable for new assets that have a recovery period of 20 years or less.[9] Nonresidential leasehold improvement for buildings that are more than three years old may also qualify for the allowance. Several restrictions apply, including exclusions of the allowance for improvements that enlarge the building or benefit a common area.[10]

> **TAX PLANNING:** Qualifying active real estate investors who anticipate that they may not be able to deduct losses several years in the future because their MAGI will exceed allowable limits may want to consider taking

---

[7] Code Sec. 469.
[8] Code Sec. 168(k) as amended by JGTRRA.
[9] Code Sec. 168(k)(2)(A)(i)(I).
[10] Code Sec. 168(k)(3).

advantage of the opportunity to use 50 percent bonus depreciation during the window, even if they cannot use all of the benefits in the current year. A taxpayer, for example, might invest in qualifying depreciable property in 2004 that would generate losses that she could not fully deduct until 2006. Such a strategy could be beneficial if the taxpayer anticipates that she would not qualify for full deduction of losses in years after 2006, because of excessive modified adjusted gross income.

Qualifying active real estate investors who invest in nonresidential real property may further benefit by investing in qualified leasehold improvements.

.02 Determining When and When Not to Utilize Rental Properties

In many and perhaps most cases, the allowance for deducting losses from rental real estate will not provide sufficient incremental benefits to induce taxpayers to choose it as an investment option. The opportunity to shelter income is essentially provided by depreciation, which for rental property, must be claimed over a 27.5 year period. Since only real property, not land, qualifies for depreciation, the current after-tax benefit may be modest, relative to the cost of the investment.

> **Example 4:** Sam and Sandra Morris purchase a house at a cost of $200,000 to be used for rental purposes. Twenty-five percent of the purchase cost is attributable to the land. Their annual allowable annual depreciation allowance will be $5,455 [$150,000/27.5 years]. If the taxpayers are in the 25 percent tax bracket, the current tax savings will be $1,364. A significant portion of this tax benefit, however, must be recaptured, at capital gains rates, at the time of the sale.

Another deterrent to using rental property for sheltering income is that the allowable income limit for claiming rental losses is not adjusted for inflation.

> **Example 5:** Helen Smith, who has an adjusted gross income of $120,000 purchases a rental property in 2000. In that year the maximum amount she may claim as a loss is $15,000. If her adjusted gross income were to increase at a rate of 5 percent per year the maximum amount she would be able to claim yearly would be limited as follows:

Year	AGI	Maximum Loss Allowance
2001	126,000	$12,000
2002	132,300	8,850
2003	138,915	5,543
2004	145,861	2,070
2005	153,154	-0-

¶403 Rental of a Personal Residence Prior to Sale May Allow Taxpayers to Claim Losses for Otherwise Nondeductible Costs

In some cases, rental of a personal residence prior to its sale may allow individuals to effectively claim losses for costs that would not otherwise be deductible.

Example 6: Fran Neville owns a personal residence that she purchased several years earlier at a cost of $210,000. The current value of the house is $200,000. She anticipates that net proceeds from the sale of the house would be reduced by $14,000 for realtor commissions and $6,000 for other costs (e.g., transfer taxes and fixing-up expenses).

Scenario 1

Fran immediately sells the property for a price of $200,000 and receives $180,000 after incurring $20,000 in closing and fixing-up costs. Her total loss is $30,000, none of which is deductible.

Scenario 2

Same as Scenario 1 except that the property is sold after being rented for one year. Assuming the property qualifies as rental property, she is able to claim a capital loss of $20,000. The $10,000 decline in value for the property prior to its placement in service is still nondeductible.

Note: This scenario assumes no depreciation claimed. If depreciation had been claimed, however, the taxpayer would have received the benefit of using it to reduce ordinary income, while having the recapture amount offset the earlier loss.

TAX PLANNING: Taxpayers may also hedge their risks by holding their former residence as a rental property for up to three years before selling it. If the property recovers its value and generates a gain, the taxpayer is still eligible to avoid recognition of income up to $250,000 ($500,000 married filing jointly) under the provisions of Section 121, providing for exclusion of gain on the sale of a personal residence. Any realized gain, however, attributable to depreciation is not eligible for exclusion.

Scenario 3

Fran rents the property for three years and sells it for a price of $250,000 and receives $230,000 after incurring $20,000 in closing costs. In the three years she has rented the property, she claimed $12,000 in depreciation expense. Upon sale of the house she must include $12,000 in income, but no other gain is recognized, assuming the provisions of Section 121 are met. Generally, the provisions of Section 121 are met where the individual has owned and occupied a property as a principle residence for two out of the five preceding years.

.01 Planning with Rental Losses to Meet Threshold Requirements

Rental losses, allowed as deductions from gross income rather than from AGI, may allow taxpayers to meet thresholds for individual retirement account contributions and rollovers, to avoid inclusion of Social Security benefits, and/or to qualify for certain credits.

Example 7: Andy and Andrea Mitchell would like to roll over their traditional IRA into a Roth IRA, but their adjusted gross income of $110,000 exceeds the $100,000 maximum threshold. The couple could use rental losses as a means of reducing their taxable income to qualify for an allowable rollover.

Example 8: Ed and Ella Silverstein have adjusted gross income of $120,000 and $4,000 in student loan interest. If no other items are claimed to reduce AGI, the maximum allowable deduction would be $833. If an additional $10,000 in reductions to AGI were claimed, however, the amount of the deduction could be doubled.

PRACTICE POINTER: The benefits discussed above and others, such as the ability to claim increased medical deductions, may provide an impetus for individuals who are already predisposed towards making a rental real estate investment and whose income is at or near the optimal level. These benefits, however, in most cases will be relatively modest and, therefore may provide more peripheral than central consideration in the determination of whether to invest in a real estate property.

¶404 Conservation Easements Can Provide Income, Property and Estate Tax Benefits

Donations of conservation easements to qualified organizations can potentially provide significant income, property, and estate tax benefits. Opportunities to employ conservation easements, once essentially limited to large property owners, in some cases are now available for owners of parcels of land as small as once acre, depending upon the location. In the area of Cape Cod, Massachusetts, for example, it may be possible for property of almost any size to be eligible for a tax-qualifying easement.[11]

A conservation easement typically provides that a landowner transfers his development rights, in perpetuity, to a charitable organization or government agency. The land then must be used for a conservation purpose, as defined under Code Sec. 170(h)(4)(A). While some qualifying purposes, such as preservation for the general public's recreation, may require allowing access to the property to the public, others, such as providing open space or protecting the habitat of plants or wildlife, may cause no change for the landowner regarding the existing use of the property. Further, if the land is used as a farm, the owner may continue to operate it as such, while still receiving a deduction for a charitable easement.

The following example illustrates how an individual may achieve income, property, and estate tax savings through the donation of a charitable easement.

Example 9: Lisa Jennings owns a house and ten acres of undeveloped land abutting a river that she had purchased in 1970 at a cost of $50,000. Similar properties have recently been sold to developers for $500,000. Lisa transfers the development rights to a qualified charitable organization. The property's value, following the transfer to the charitable organization drops

---

[11] According to Mark H. Robinson, executive director of the Compact of Cape Cod Conservation Trusts, as reported in "Conservation Easements Lighten Taxes," by Lynn Asinof, *The Wall Street Journal*, August 1, 1999, C1.

to $150,000. As a result of this transaction, Lisa receives the following tax benefits:

A charitable deduction for appreciated property of $350,000. The amount allowed each year is limited to 30 percent of adjusted gross income, with the balance being carried forward.

A reduction in property taxes resulting from the decrease in the value of the property

A decrease in estate tax liability, after death, reflecting the decrease in the value of the property

Additionally, if she sells the property before she dies, she may be able to use up to $250,000 in exclusion from taxable income for the sale of a principal residence.

PRACTICE POINTER: Donations of charitable easements may be particularly attractive for owners of undeveloped land who:

1. Are planning to hold the property in its undeveloped state until death or as long as they remain healthy enough to maintain the property, and

2. Are more concerned about receiving current tax benefits (e.g., charitable deduction and reduced property taxes) than providing the maximum after-tax inheritance for their beneficiaries.

TAX PLANNING: Contributions, by trust, of conservation easements will qualify for charitable deductions only in cases where they are made from gross trust income and not from trust principal.[12] Direct contributions by individuals, rather than through trusts may, therefore, often be the more viable way of achieving a charitable deduction for the donation of a charitable easement.

.01 Methods of Valuation

In most cases, valuations of easements will be based on before and after valuations of a property. The valuations, in general, are based on a property's highest and best use.[13] An isolated exception to the highest and best use criteria was issued, however, in *McLennan v. Commissioner*, where the claims court held that the "before" and "after" valuations should not be based on maximum development potential because the taxpayer had a strong aversion to development.[14] If there has been a sale of a comparable easement, however, it should be used in determining valuation.[15]

PRACTICE POINTER: Clients should be advised that in the event of a valuation dispute with the IRS, the credibility and persuasiveness of the expert appraiser is critical. In *Schapiro v. Commissioner*,[16] for example, the tax court ruled in favor of the taxpayer's appraiser, who argued that the prop-

---

[12] Rev. Rul. 2003-123, 2003-50 IRB 1200.
[13] T.C. Memo 1990-242.
[14] 24 Cl. Ct. 102 (1991).
[15] Reg. § 1.170A-14(h)(3)(i).
[16] T.C. Memo 1991-128.

¶404.01

erty could have been developed into ten lots, rather than the Commissioner's appraiser, who argued that the property could be developed into only two lots. The court, rather than specifying its reasons for its decision said simply, "We think under the circumstances of this case that Mr. Moore's [taxpayer expert] approach is the sounder of the two."

Clients should be made aware that the courts have been moving from a "split-the-difference" approach and have been increasingly basing their decisions on the basis of the quality of the expert appraisal.[17] Any attempt, therefore, to seek out appraisers who will provide the highest rather than the soundest appraisal could potentially cause very significant damage, including additional charges for interest and penalties.

¶405 Transfer of a Personal Residence with Retained Life Estate May Provide an Opportunity to Avoid Medicaid Transfer

If an individual owns a home at the time of entering a nursing home and he or she does not have sufficient funds to cover those costs, Medicaid or other agency (e.g., county Department of Social Services), may impose a lien against the property as a means to recover them.[18] An individual may, however, potentially transfer a personal residence, while maintaining the right to use it, prior to entering the nursing home, and not have it considered an asset subject to Medicaid collection.

An individual who transfers property with a retained life estate generally has the right to occupy and enjoy the property, including the right to collect rent, while he or she is alive. At death, the transferor loses all rights to the property and the beneficiaries, therefore, obtain full rights to the property without going through the probate process. The benefit, for Medicaid purposes, typically is that the property is transferred to the beneficiaries without being used to cover long-term costs. Although the full value of the property is required to be included in the value of the estate at death, it is unlikely that an individual who qualifies for Medicaid will have an estate that is actually subject to estate taxes.[19] Similarly, the fact that the annual exclusion is not allowed for gifts of future interests is also not likely to be an issue.[20]

---

[17] This trend and other issues of easement valuation are well discussed in "Understanding the Evolution of Conservation Easement Appraisal through Case Law," by Craig L. Byrne and Michael Minck in *Appraisal Journal*, October 2000, Vol. 68, Issue 4, pp. 411-419.

[18] A fuller discussion is contained in "Planning Protects the Family Home," by Lawrence Eric Davidow, *New York Law Journal*, May 21, 2001, p. 9-13.

[19] Code Sec. 2036, "Transfers with Retained Life Estate," provides that the value of the gross estate includes the value of all property where the individual had the right to possession, enjoyment, or income from until the date of death.

[20] Reg. §25.2503-3.

¶406 Qualified Exchange Accommodation Arrangements (QEAAs) May Provide Safe Harbors for Reverse Like-Kind Exchanges

Although owners of real estate can potentially benefit from deferral of gains through like-kind exchanges, complex and restrictive regulations may have prevented some taxpayers from engaging in reverse exchanges,[21] whereby replacement property is acquired before the sale of the relinquished property. The issuance of Rev. Proc. 2000-37,[22] however, by providing answers to the following three previously unresolved questions, provides a safe harbor for those taxpayers considering entering into such transactions.

1. Is a direct transfer of the replacement property required or may interrelated transactions through an intermediary be used?

2. How does the requirement that replacement property be identified not more than 180 days after the day of transfer apply in cases where it has been acquired *before* the transfer?

3. At what point does the 180-day period begin to run?[23]

Rev. Proc. 2000-37 provides answers to these questions and, accordingly, a safe harbor for taxpayers considering entering into reverse exchange transactions.

1. Interrelated transactions are allowable. Property must be held by an *exchange accommodation titleholder (EAT)*, an individual or entity who is not the taxpayer or a disqualified person.

2. The relinquished property must be identified within 45 days after the transfer of the replacement property.

3. A combined 180-day period is the maximum time that the relinquished and replacement property can be held within a QEAA. Additionally, within 180 days after transfer to the EAT, the property must be a) transferred (either directly or indirectly through a qualified intermediary) to the taxpayer as the replacement property or b) transferred to a person who is not taxpayer or disqualified person as relinquished property.

Additional rules apply in order for the transaction to meet the safe harbor of Rev. Proc. 2000-37, including a requirement that within five days the EAT and the taxpayer enter into a written agreement detailing compliance with the revenue procedure.[24]

---

[21] These exchanges are also known as reverse-Starker exchanges, *Starker*, 602 F.2d 1341 (CA-9, 1979).

[22] Rev. Proc. 2000-37, 2000-40 IRB 308.

[23] These three questions, their historical application, and current application are presented and discussed in a more comprehensive analysis than presented in this text in "Deferred Reverse Like-Kind Exchanges," by J.W. Burgess and William L. Raby, *Tax Notes*, Vol. 89, October 23, 2000, pp. 521-528. *See also* "Gains and Losses: Rev. Proc. 2000-37 Offers Long-Awaited Reverse-Exchange Safe Harbor," by James R. Hamill, *The Tax Adviser*, Vol. 190, March 2001.

[24] The detailed requirements are contained within Rev. Proc. 2000-37.

TAX PLANNING: Like-kind exchanges of real estate, in addition to providing current income tax deferral, can potentially provide significant estate tax benefits. The unrecognized gains may in some cases never be recognized, depending upon when the decedent dies and/or the amount of appreciation of property within the estate.[25] Although the full value of the property is subject to estate tax, liquidation of the property may not be required in cases where life insurance is held by a third party, such as an irrevocable life insurance trust (ILIT).[26] If properly structured, the proceeds from the life insurance can be excluded from the estate.[27]

PRACTICE POINTER: In a "hot" real estate market any delay in entering into a purchase agreement, such as that arising from an investor identifying and then transferring property to an intermediary, could potentially result in a lost investment opportunity. Reverse like-kind exchanges can be particularly beneficial in such situations by eliminating or reducing delays in closing on the replacement property.

PRACTICE POINTER: Any deferred exchange that does not use a qualified intermediary may be a major audit target. Such disqualified intermediaries may include related parties and agents of the taxpayer, such as her accountants or attorneys.[28]

---

[25] While the tax-free step-up in basis provisions are scheduled to expire for decedents dying after December 31, 2009, executors, after that date will be able to step up basis by $1,300,000 or $3,000,000 for a surviving spouse.

[26] In order to exclude insurance proceeds from the gross estate, the insured normally cannot have the power to revoke, amend or alter. A more detailed discussion of irrevocable life insurance trusts is contained in "Irrevocable Life Insurance Trust and Variable Life Insurance," by Jennifer Roper and Randy L. Zipse, *Adviser Today*, Vol. 96, Issue 2, February 2001, pp. 64-66.

[27] A more detailed discussion of this topic is contained in "Estate Planning Benefits of Deferred Like-Kind Exchanges of Real Estate," by Myron Kove and James M. Kosakow, *Estate Planning*, Volume 28, August 2001.

[28] This issue and others relating to audit risk for like-kind exchanges are discussed in "What the Deferred Exchange Regulations Forgot to Tell You: How the Internal Revenue Service Will Audit a Section 1031 Exchange," by Terence Floyd Cuff, *The Journal of Real Estate Taxation*, Vol. 21-173, Winter 1994. Although some aspects of the law have changed since the publication of this article, it still contains many potentially helpful pointers on how to properly structure a like-kind exchange in order to avoid its disallowance by the Internal Revenue Service.

Chapter 5

DERIVATIVES

¶501 Overview—Operation, Benefits and Risks

Investors who are considering using options and other derivatives for purposes other than hedging risk and/or obtaining modest tax deferral benefits should be cognizant of the high risk that these investments entail. Long Term Capital Management, a hedge fund staffed with some of the most highly regarded financial talent, including Nobel Prize winners, achieved great notoriety for the enormity of their losses. Jane Bryant Quinn, nationally syndicated financial columnist states simply, "No individual seriously trying to build wealth should use options, period."[1]

While the use of options may be potentially hazardous for wealth building, they may be beneficial for reducing risk and/or deferring taxable gain, particularly when used in a "covered call" transaction or together with puts in transactions referred to as "collars." The basic operation and tax treatment of calls, puts, as well as related futures oriented investments, regulated futures contracts and forward contracts are discussed below. Also discussed are "straddles," where holdings of offsetting positions result in a "substantial diminution of risk," resulting in a suspension of holding periods and/or deferral of otherwise recognizable loss.

Calls: provide the right to purchase an investment at a particular price during a particular time period. The rights are normally for 100 shares of stock. "In-the-money" calls refer to calls where the right to purchase price is less than the current market price (e.g., stock price is $70 and the call's right to purchase price is $60). "Listed" calls refer to calls that are traded through an exchange (e.g., Chicago Board Options Exchange).

Since most calls expire in a period less than one year, their sale will normally result in short-term capital gain or loss treatment. If, however, the holder of the call exercises the conversion right, gain or loss on the transaction can be deferred until an actual sale or disposition of the stock. The holding period for the stock does not include the holding period of the call.

An exception to short-term capital gain treatment is potentially available for Long-Term Equity Anticipation Securities (LEAPS), that provide expirations in January of each of the next two years. LEAPS are traded on the Chicago Board Options Exchange (*www.cboe.com*).

---

[1] *Making the Most of Your Money*, by Jane Bryant Quinn, Simon & Schuster, 1997.

While calls are primarily sold by large funds and institutions, individuals can also sell these investments. A covered call is one where the investor selling the call owns the underlying stock. The potential economic benefit of selling calls is that premium income is earned in exchange for providing the buyer with the right to purchase stock at a designated price. If the call is not exercised, the seller receives the full benefit of the premium. Economic detriments of selling calls are:

1. Lack of opportunity for full upside gain, and

2. Only modest protection (premium received) where the value of the underlying stock falls.

A potential tax deferral benefit of selling calls is that gains or losses are not recognized until the option is closed or expires.[2]

Investors may be able to obtain some relief from the anti-straddle rules (discussed below) through the use of *qualified* covered call options. These rules allow investors to benefit from the use of offsetting positions, with only relatively modest levels of risk.

Puts: provide the right to sell an investment at a particular price during a particular time period. Also, similarly to calls, normally sold in rights for 100 shares of stock. "In-the-money," puts refers to puts where the right to sell price is greater than the current market price (e.g., put right to sell price is $70 and stock price is $60).

Straddle: the use of identical or substantially identical offsetting positions that, without restrictions, would allow taxpayers:

1. To recognize current losses while deferring gain,

2. Extend holding periods, or

3. Incurring significant risk of diminution of investment.[3]

Detriments of a transaction being categorized as a straddle include:

1. Losses being deferred for tax purposes, and

2. Interest expense incurred to carry the position being categorized as capital expenses.

Forward contract: the obligation to purchase a commodity, including currencies, at a specified date and price. Generally, the sale of appreciated property already owned or substantially identical to it by the taxpayer for delivery at a future date is treated as a constructive sale. Some exceptions apply for debt instruments, instruments subject to the mark-to-market rule, and where instruments are not readily marketable and the position is closed within one year.[4]

Regulated futures contract: contracts for the future sale/purchase of commodities, traded on or subject to the rules of a qualified exchange. Contracts are marked to market, with all contracts held at the end of the year, treated as if sold on that day. Gains and loss are subject to the 60/40 rule, whereby 60 percent of

---

[2] Code Sec. 1234(b).   [4] Code Sec. 1259.
[3] Code Sec. 1092.

¶501

gains and losses are treated as long-term and 40 percent are treated as short-term, regardless of holding period.[5] An additional potential tax benefit of regulated futures contracts, in addition to having otherwise short-term gains treated as 60 percent long-term gains, is that current losses can be elected to be carried back three years to offset gains from such contracts.[6]

PRACTICE POINTER: The relatively modest tax benefits of regulated futures contracts (i.e., 60/40 rule and loss carryback opportunities) for most taxpayers will not provide sufficient benefits to outweigh the risks of these investments. Clients considering investing in regulated futures contracts should be alerted to their potentially high level of risk, particularly in cases where prices are subject to rapid changes based on external factors (e.g., orange juice prices subject to changes in weather conditions or oil prices subject to changes in foreign government leadership).

¶502 Covered Calls Can Allow for Potential Deferral of Gain with Modest Risk

An individual holding stock, who seeks to defer recognition of gain until the following period, may benefit from the use of an offsetting covered call option. In general, offsetting positions of a qualified call option and its underlying stock are not treated as a straddle, where the offsetting positions are not part of a larger straddle.[7]

A covered call option is defined as one that meets the following requirements:[8]

- option is traded on an exchange registered with the SEC or other market deemed adequate by the Secretary
- option is granted more than thirty days before it expires
- option is not a deep-in-the money option
- underlying stock is either already owned by the taxpayer or acquired in connection with the option

The actual lowest qualifying strike price will vary depending upon the previous closing day's stock price and whether there are more than 90 days until the call's expiration. In all cases, a qualifying covered call must have more than 30 days until expiration.

Example 1: Pat Albert holds 1,000 shares of ABC Corporation that she purchased a number of years ago at $30/share. The closing price of the stock for the previous day was $73. Although income on the sale of the stock would result in favorable long-term capital gain treatment, she would prefer not to recognize it currently because an increase in current adjusted gross income would result in her losing eligibility for the Hope Education Credit. Pat, through the use of a qualified cover may potentially:

---

[5] Code Sec. 1256.
[6] Code Sec. 1212(c).

[7] Code Sec. 1092(c)(4)(A).
[8] Code Sec. 1092(c)(4)(B).

1. Defer gain, subject to a reduced level of risk, and

2. Generate premium income.

Pat issues a call option for $10 with an expiration of 31-90 days. The call's right-to-purchase price is $70, the lowest qualifying strike price available for a call of that term,[9] assuming $5 price intervals. Her potential income and losses are as follows:

Stock's price > $73. Income is fixed at $7,000. Premium of $10 is offset by call purchaser's $3 in-the-money gain. Alice has no potential to benefit from appreciation in value of stock.

Stock price between $70 and $73. Income is fixed at $7,000. Since option price is fixed at 70, any exercise at 70 would reflect a $3,000 loss in the underlying value of the stock.

Stock price between $63 and $70. Income of $7,000, from writing calls would be reduced by $1,000 for each dollar drop in the value of the underlying stock. At a price of 63, the taxpayer is at a breakeven point (i.e., $10,000 premium income is offset by $10,000 decline in value of shares).

Note: Option would expire unexercised.

Stock price below $63. Actual losses would be incurred of $1,000 for each dollar drop in the value of the underlying stock below $63.

Note: Option would expire unexercised.

Note that the holding period of the underlying stock is suspended during the period that the call is outstanding.[10]

TAX PLANNING: Covered call option, however, will not be excluded from straddle treatment in cases where the grantor holds a put option on the same underlying equity.[11]

.01 FLEX and Over-the-Counter Options May Also Qualify for Covered Call Treatments

The Service has issued regulations that extend covered call treatment for certain FLEX equity and over-the-counter options for options written on or after July 29, 2002.[12] The use of OTC equity derivatives has grown significantly over recent years.[13]

¶503 Zero Premium Collars Provide Opportunities to Defer Gain and Hedge Risk

Investors may potentially defer gain and hedge risk through the use of zero premium collars. Zero premium collars are normally comprised of a set of an out-of-the-money put and an out-of-the-money call that cover the same underly-

---

[9] Code Sec. 1092(c)(4)(D).
[10] Code Sec. 1092(f)(2).
[11] Rev. Rul. 2002-66.
[12] Reg. § 1.1092(c).

[13] "Product Gives Stock Exposure at Limited Risk – OTC Equity Derivatives are a Hit with Investors, Profitable for Brokers," by Paula Froelich, *Wall Street Journal*, July 26, p. B8.

ing stock. The premium that the shareholder receives for writing the call, relinquishing the opportunity for upside appreciation, is used to purchase a put, providing protection against a decline in the stock's market value. Investors may also invest in collars where premiums earned are more or less than the amount paid for acquisition of puts.

The spread between a collar's put and call price is generally referred to as its "width" and is referred to in terms of the percentage of the value of the asset at the time it is issued (e.g., a 95-110 collar, refers to a collar with an exercisable put price of 95 percent of the asset's value and a call with a sale price of 110 percent of its value).[14]

Example 2: Bob Alpha, who owns stock in ABC Corporation currently trading at 100, acquires a collar comprised of a 90 put and a 115 call. The proceeds from selling the call cover the cost of the purchase of the put. As a result of this transaction, Bob's potential upside appreciation is capped at a price of 115, while his potential for loss is limited to a price of 90. This transaction allows the investor to lock in most of his gain, potentially achieve limited upside appreciation, and defer gain recognition for the underlying stock.

A concern in acquiring collars for the purposes of locking in and deferring gain is that the collar's width must be sufficiently large to avoid constructive sale treatment for the underlying stock.[15] The IRS is authorized, but has not yet issued regulations providing specific standards delineating when a collar will be subject to constructive sale treatment. Committee reports have indicated that factors to be considered should include:

1. The spread between the put and call strike prices,

2. Duration of the collar, and

3. Right to periodic payments (e.g., dividends). A ten percent minimum spread for each of the put and call sides seems to be the current rule of thumb used in the financial community.[16]

---

[14] "Recommendations for the Forthcoming Constructive Sales Regulations," by the American Bar Association Section of Taxation, *Tax Notes*, Vol. 92, p. 1719, September 24, 2001.

[15] Code Sec. 1259(c)(1).

[16] According to "Making the Most of the Capital Gains Tax Cut," by Janet Novack, *Forbes*, September 8, 1997, pages 202-204, " . . . most experts think that strike prices spaced 10 percent away form the current price will do." Similarly, according to "Constructive Sales Treatment for Appreciated Financial Positions," by Jeffrey Palley, *The Tax Adviser*, June 2000, p. 394, "Wall Street usually uses 10 percent

risk as a guideline to avoid the constructive sale rules. As long as both the upside and downside potential are at least 10 percent, it presumes that the constructive sales rules will not be triggered." The American Bar Association recommends, should the IRS choose to adopt a simple approach, that 20 be used as an acceptable width for five year collars. They believe it may be preferable, however, to adopt a more flexible approach that prescribes different acceptable collar widths for different periods to maturity ["Recommendations for the Forthcoming Constructive Sales Regulations," by the American Bar Association Section of Taxation, *Tax Notes*, September 24, 2001, p. 1719].

¶504 Incentive Stock Options Offer Planning Opportunities but Pose Hazards

Qualified incentive stock options can potentially provide employees with the opportunity to purchase stock at a discounted price and then recognize income upon disposition at capital gains rates. Generally, the employee must hold the option for at least two years and the stock, itself, for at least one year to qualify for this favorable treatment. If stock purchased is not held for the requisite period then the "spread," the difference on the exercise date between the stock's fair market value and purchase price, is treated as compensation, subject to ordinary income rates and payroll taxes.

While no income, for regular tax purposes, is recognized at the time of exercise, the spread between the purchase and market price is subject to inclusion in alternative minimum taxable income. A potential risk for the taxpayer is that the value of the stock can decline, after exercise, resulting in the taxpayer being subject to AMT, without the wherewithal to pay the tax. In the years 2000 and 2001, this risk became a reality for a number of individuals in the technology and Internet sectors.

Potential methods to reduce the hazard of alternative minimum tax include:[17]

1. **Limit the number of shares exercised to minimize AMT exposure.** A client, particularly in situations where the options are exercised near year-end, can prepare pro-forma computations to determine the amount of shares that can be exercised without incurring AMT. The client could also, effectively, hedge, by exercising and disposing of some shares, resulting in the recognition of ordinary income. The recognition of some additional ordinary income may allow additional shares to be exercised without application of the AMT.

   TAX PLANNING: The taxpayer may wish to implement this strategy only to the extent that it does not cause her to shift into a higher ordinary tax bracket. This strategy is more effective where the spread between capital gains rates and ordinary income rates is low and the taxpayer is not subject to Social Security taxes on the recognized income.

2. **In a declining market, sell shares through a "disqualifying disposition," prior to the end of the year in which the stock was acquired.** A disqualifying disposition occurs in cases where the stock is sold prior to meeting the required holding periods and results in treatment similar to that of nonqualified stock options under Code Sec. 422(a)(1).

   Example 3: Jack Mosely, on January 15, 2004, exercises 10,000 incentive stock options of Mighty Corp. at $15/share. The fair market value of the stock at the time is $35/share. At December 31, 2004, Jack sells the shares at Mighty Corp.'s current market value of $17/share.

---

[17] Additional information on this topic is contained in "ISOs and the AMT" by Mark Topolski, Joseph Aleshire, and Cindie Rosenzweig, in *The Tax Adviser*, April 2001, p. 248.

As a result of this transaction Jack:

1. Recognizes ordinary income of $20,000 [10,000 shares x ($17 sales price - $15 exercise price], and

2. Incurs no net AMT adjustment, since the amount of regular income recognized equals the amount of the AMT adjustment.

The importance of selling the shares in the same year is illustrated by the following example:

Example 4: Same facts as in the previous example except that the stock is sold January 2, 2005.

As a result of this transaction Jack:

1. Recognizes no ordinary income in 2004,

2. Recognizes a $200,000 AMT adjustment in 2004,

3. Recognizes $20,000 ordinary income in 2005, and

4. Realizes an AMT short-term capital loss of $180,000 in 2005; the loss can only be used to offset AMT capital gains and $3,000 of other income.

In cases where the stock's value has declined beyond the purchase price, there is no recognition of compensation income.

Example 5: Same facts as in Example 3, except that the stock is sold December 31, 2004 for $12/share.

As a result of this transaction Jack:

1. Recognizes no ordinary income; under Code Sec. 422(c)(2) taxable compensation is not recognized where there is a disqualifying disposition and the amount realized is less than the value at exercise, and

2. Realizes a short-term capital loss of $30,000 [10,000 shares x ($15 - $12)], recognized to the extent of his total net capital gains and $3,000 ordinary income.

PRACTICE POINTER: The three examples above illustrate how highly important it is to monitor performance of exercised stock options prior to year end. Also, if possible, exercise of options at the beginning of the year may reduce the period of time that a taxpayer is at risk prior to reaching the capital gains rates holding period. Similarly, if options are exercisable near year-end, pro-forma calculations may be conducted to determine the maximum amount that can be exercised without triggering the AMT.

.01 ISO Section 83(b) Election for Alternative Minimum Tax Purposes May Reduce Total Alternative Minimum Tax

While Section 83(b) elections are not allowed for purposes of computing regular tax on the exercise of an ISO,[18] taxpayers may make this election for

---

[18] Code Sec. 83(e)(1).

purposes of the alternative minimum tax.[19] A section 83(b) election, discussed in more detail in the next section, results in immediate recognition of income, reflecting the difference between the stock's fair market value and the option's exercise price, reduced by any amount paid for the option itself.

This election may be beneficial in cases where a taxpayer can absorb additional alternative minimum taxable income in the current year without actually triggering alternative minimum tax liability. The current recognition of untaxed AMT income can act to reduce the amount of income potentially subject to AMT in future years.

¶505 Section 83(b) Provides an Opportunity to Convert Ordinary Income from Nonqualified Stock Options (NQSO) to Capital Gains, but with Potentially Significant Risks

Section 83(b) provides an opportunity for some taxpayers, through an election, to potentially convert ordinary income, resulting from the appreciation of nonqualified stock options, into capital gains. While, under Section 83, a taxpayer holding NQSOs normally recognizes ordinary income at the time the stock first becomes either transferable or is no longer subject to significant risk of forfeiture,[20] a taxpayer may elect to recognize ordinary income immediately upon receipt of the restricted property.[21] Any further change in value is treated as capital gain or loss.

A potentially significant risk of making a Section 83(b) election is that if the stock falls in value prior to vesting, the taxpayer may have to recognize ordinary income, but 1) lack cash to pay that tax and/or 2) incur excessive capital losses that may not be currently deductible.

> **PRACTICE POINTER:** The section 83(b) election may be most attractive for taxpayers who are in higher marginal tax brackets and also typically generate capital gains (e.g., frequent traders). The higher marginal bracket taxpayer potentially benefits more because the spread between marginal ordinary income rates (e.g., 35 percent) and long-term capital gains rates (e.g., 15 percent) is greater than that for taxpayers in lower marginal tax brackets.

Individuals who typically generate capital gains can potentially receive at least a partial benefit from the section 83(b) election, even if the value of the stock underlying the NQSO declines, because it can be used as an offset against the taxpayer's other capital gain income. The election may be even more attractive in cases where the taxpayer is expected to incur short-term capital gains because, even if the stock declines in value, it can be used to offset capital gains that are

---

[19] Code Sec. 56(b)(3) provides that incentive stock rules do not apply for purposes of the alternative minimum tax. Also, IRS Information Letter, INFO 2001-0224, released September 28, 2001, states that, "for AMT purposes only, a Code Sec. 83(b) election may be made for substantially nonvested incentive stock option stock (p.2)."

[20] The amount of ordinary income is based on the difference between the FMV of the stock and the exercise price, at the time the property is no longer subject to the restrictions.

[21] Code Sec. 83(b)(2) provides that the election must be made not later than thirty days after the date of such transfer.

taxed at a taxpayer's ordinary income tax rate, rather than at the reduced long-term capital gains rate.

Example 6: Bob, a taxpayer subject to an ordinary marginal tax bracket of 35 percent elects, under Section 83(b), to immediately recognize income on currently nontransferable NQSOs. Bob immediately recognizes ordinary income of $100,000. Just over one year later, after the transferability restrictions expire, Bob sells the stock and recognizes capital gain on the appreciation of another $100,000. Whereas the first $100,000 in income is subject to tax at a 35 percent rate, the second $100,000 in income, treated as a long-term capital gain, is subject to tax at only a 15 percent rate. If no election had been made, all of the income would have been taxable at a 35 percent rate.

The next example, illustrates the potential attractiveness of the Section 83(b) election to an individual who is a frequent trader and has or may be expected to generate short-term capital gains.

Example 7: Same facts as in Example 6, except that Bob loses $100,000 on the NQSOs while also generating $100,000 in short-term capital gains from stock trading activities. Bob still recognizes $100,000 in ordinary income at a 35 percent rate, but the loss from the NQSOs offsets the income from the short-term capital gains at the same 35 percent rate. Therefore, despite a decline in stock value following the election, Bob essentially fares no worse than in the event that he had not made the election.[22]

Alternatively, if in fact Bob did not generate capital gains, he would only be allowed to currently deduct $3,000 in capital losses, with the remainder being carried forward for use in future years, but again subject to the maximum allowance of only $3,000/year.

¶506 Transfers of Nonqualified Stock Options (NQSOs) to Family Members May Provide Significant Tax Benefits

In cases where plans allow nonqualified stock options to be transferred to family members,[23] an opportunity may be available to shift rapidly appreciating assets outside of an individual's taxable estate. This option may be particularly desirable in situations where there is a high expectation that the value of nonqualified stock options will appreciate at a rate in excess of other assets that potentially could be used for family gifts. Such an expectation may be reasonable, for example, in cases where an executive's compensation is based largely on the amount of appreciation in his company's stock.

The benefit of this transfer may be reduced, however, in cases where the taxpayer must render additional services before being allowed to exercise the option. Rev. Rul. 98-21[24] provides that where additional services are a condition to vesting, a completed gift will not be recognized until those services are

---

[22] Bob does, however, recognize income from the Code Sec. 83(b) election one year before he receives the benefit of the loss in the NQSO's value.

[23] Prior to November 1996, the SEC required that such options be nontransferable. Some companies may still have clauses that prevent transfer of these options.

[24] Rev. Rul. 98-21, 1998-18 IRB 7.

completed. Nonetheless, even under this condition, some taxpayers may find that opportunities for continued appreciation, after vesting but prior to exercise, may still be strong and, therefore, make transfers of nonqualified stock options an attractive option for family gifts.

PRACTICE POINTER: Although a gift of nonqualified stock options is deemed complete at the time of vesting, the transferor is still required to recognize taxable income at the time of exercise. Therefore, clients should be advised that in the year of exercise they will be subject to tax on the income earned, but will not be receiving cash for its payment.

PRACTICE POINTER: Transfers of options to family members may also be made through trusts. Such transfers, in order to be treated as completed gifts, should follow the rules applicable to irrevocable transfers to trusts, including the requirement that the transferor not retain power over the disposition of the trust's property. The rule requiring vesting by the transferor before there is treatment as a completed gift is still applicable.

Chapter 6

ANNUITIES

¶601 Variable Annuities—In General

Variable annuities are tax-deferred investment vehicles that contain insurance features. A basic variable annuity contract will hold a mutual fund investment and carry a death benefit protecting the investor's principal. A more feature laden annuity may contain a death benefit that guarantees payment equal to the annuity's highest anniversary value and/or a living benefit that provides a minimum guaranteed gain. In general, as more benefits are added the greater become the costs of the annuity.

The primary benefits of variable annuities are as follows:

- Earnings accumulate tax-deferred until withdrawn,
- Tax-free transfers can be made among the issuer's investments,
- No limitations are placed on the amount of allowed contributions, and
- Death benefits may be provided for protection of principal.

Despite these benefits, variable annuities are often not a primary choice for investing for a variety of reasons including the following:

- Contributions, unlike those for qualified retirement plans, are made with after-tax, rather than pre-tax dollars,
- Distributions of income, unlike those from Roth IRAs, are subject to taxation,
- Income distributed, despite a long-term holding of principal, is subject to tax at ordinary income rates,
- Costs are often substantial as compared to those for acquiring and holding stocks and mutual funds[1], and
- Surrender periods may be significantly long so as to effectively limit liquidity.

> **TAX PLANNING:** Variable annuities may be beneficial, from a tax perspective, in cases where the preponderance of income generated from the investment would be ordinary (e.g., REITS) and the taxpayer does not have availability for its holding in a tax-deferred or tax-exempt account (e.g., Roth IRA). If, however, significant acquisition costs, operating ex-

---

[1] The average annual expenses for a variable annuity are 2.23 percent, per Variable Annuity Research & Data Services (VARDS) as reported in "The Fifth Best Option," by Christopher Farrell, *Business Week*, May 8, 2000, pp. 166-168.

penses, or surrender charges apply, then such an investment, from an overall financial planning perspective, may prove less attractive.[2]

.01 Life Insurance Feature—Cost/Benefit

When evaluating the cost-benefit of a variable annuity's life insurance feature, one should consider the mortality risk of the investor and the type of investment that is being protected. Although the costs of this benefit can be significant, average annual cost of 1.18 percent,[3] less than one half of one percent of variable annuities are paid out due to death or disability.[4] Further, it is likely that many of these payments contained no life insurance benefit because the value of the investment at date of death was greater than it was at the most recent valuation date. In some cases, perhaps an older investor purchasing investments in a volatile market (e.g., emerging markets), the insurance may be cost-effective. If the investor is too old, however, there may be limits on the payments of insurance. Some policies, for example, provide for expiration of the death benefit at ages 75 or 80.

> **PRACTICE POINTER:** If an investor is concerned about maintaining the value of principal in event of death, it may be more cost effective to purchase some term insurance and/or vary investments within the portfolio. An investor, for example, could reduce the volatility of stock holdings by purchasing some convertible stocks, which may have a low correlation to stocks, and/or purchasing inflation adjusted bonds (I-bonds), which are guaranteed not to lose value beyond principal.

¶602 Alternatives to Variable Annuities

Investors who are saving money for retirement generally should maximize contributions to qualified retirement accounts and Roth IRAs before contributing to variable annuities. Contributions to qualified retirement accounts can be made with pre-tax, rather than after-tax dollars, as are required with annuity investments. Roth IRAs, while similarly to variable annuities require after-tax contributions,[5] provide the benefit of tax-free distributions.

After an investor has maximized contributions to qualified retirement accounts and Roth IRAs, the following additional tax-saving alternatives may also be considered:

1. **Exchange-traded funds (ETFs).** A number of exchange traded funds, such as those based on the Nasdaq 100 (Cubes) and the Standard & Poor's 500 (SPDRs) potentially provide the following benefits over varia-

---

[2] Conversations 16968 and 16975 of *Morningstar.com* contain a forum on the subject of investing in annuities, *Morningstar.com.*

[3] According to *Morningstar, Inc.,* reported in "What's Wrong with Variable Annuities," *SmartMoney.com.* 2001.

[4] According to a 1997 report by Limra International, an insurance industry research group, as reported in "What's Wrong with Variable Annuities," *SmartMoney.com* 2001.

[5] Some taxpayers who meet income requirements (i.e., joint filers with AGI of $50,000 or less, heads of households with with AGI of $37,500 or less, and others with AGIs of $25,000 or less) and other requirements (e.g., not claimed by someone else as a dependent), additionally, may qualify for credits for contributions made to Roth and/or qualified retirement accounts (Code Sec. 25B as added by the Economic Growth and Tax Relief Reconciliation Act). Such benefits are not available for purchasers of variable annuities.

ble annuities: 1) opportunities to recognize gains at preferred capital gains rates; 2) opportunities to sell shares without incurring fees for early surrender; and 3) opportunities to reduce costs for purchases and operating expenses.

The primary disadvantage of ETFs, as compared to variable annuities, is that there is not a 100 percent deferral of income. Holders of ETFs are required to recognize current dividend payments and, in some cases, a passthrough of capital gains. These amounts, however, may be so minimal (e.g., approximately 1 percent or less for dividend payments, and zero or close to zero for passthrough of gains), that they will be less than the annual operating expense imposed by some annuity issuers.

2. **Low turnover index funds.** Index funds with low turnover, such as those based on the S&P 500, provide similar benefits to ETFs. Index funds, however, can normally be bought without commissions, an advantage over ETFs, but generally will have a higher passthrough of gains and potential risk for recognition of built-in gains.

3. **Tax-managed funds.** These funds also provide opportunities for long-term deferral of gains and income recognition at preferred capital gains rates. A disadvantage of these funds is that pre-tax performance could be hampered by the parameters of tax-managed operations.

4. **I-bonds.** I-Bonds provide opportunities to defer income recognition for up to thirty years. I-bonds also provide the benefits of being free of commissions and operating expenses, while generating income that is exempt from state and local taxes. A limitation of I-bonds is that only $30,000/year for each individual may be purchased.

PRACTICE POINTER: The evaluation of whether to purchase ETFs and/or index funds, as opposed to a variable annuity, may depend upon the structure of the individual's portfolio. While the variety of low turnover index-based investments may be limited, taxpayers may still have the opportunity to maintain diversified accounts by holding offsetting investments in their tax-deferred accounts (e.g., 401-k plans), or tax-exempt accounts (Roth IRAs). A taxpayer could, for example, balance her holdings of large capitalization index-based investments (e.g., SPDRs) held in a taxable account with holdings of small capitalization managed investments in a tax-deferred or tax-exempt account.

TAX PLANNING: An investor generally should not be using variable annuities to hold investments that would already provide a high level of tax deferral. If, for example, the investor were to hold an S&P 500 index fund in a variable annuity account, he could land up paying unnecessarily high fees while converting income that would otherwise be subject to capital gain recognition into ordinary income property. Similarly, tax-exempt bonds should not be held in a variable annuity.

TAX PLANNING: Taxpayers in high tax brackets considering investing in fixed income investments, such as corporate bonds, for an annuity account should compare the costs with a low-cost municipal bond fund. Evaluation of commissions and operating expenses may be particularly critical where returns are expected to be relatively low. If, for example a bond fund is expected to yield 7 percent per year and the annuity's operating costs are 2.1 percent per year, there would be a 30 percent pre-tax reduction in return.

¶603 IRS Formula Provides Opportunity to Defer Annuity Income

A potential benefit of receiving payments through an annuity is the opportunity to receive income based on a formula that does not take into account *true* amortization of income. The amount of exclusion for each annuity payment is determined by the following formula:

$$\frac{\text{Investment (I)}}{\text{Expected Return (ER)}} \times \text{Annuity Payment (AP)} = \text{Exclusion Amount (EA)}$$

Example 1: Tom Cage, age 65, invests $500,000 in a commercial (nonqualified) annuity, with payments being made over his life expectancy. Annual cash payments are $43,592. Since the annuity is for a nonqualified plan, Tom uses the table for "Ordinary Life Annuities: One Life – Expected Return Multiples."[6] The multiple for an individual, age 65, is 20.0 years.

$$\frac{\$500,000 \text{ (I)}}{\$871,840^a \text{ (ER)}} \times \$43,592 \text{ (AP)} = \$25,000 \text{ (EA)}$$

[a] 20 Years x $43,592/year.

Annual reportable income:

$43,592	Annual Payment
$25,000	Exclusion Amount
$18,592	Annual Reportable Income

Year	Compound Interest Earned	Current Year Tax Reportable Interest	Deferred Earned Interest
1	$30,00 [a]	$18,592	$11,408
2	29,184	18,592	10,592
3	28,320	18,592	9,728
4	27,404	18,592	8,812
5	26,432	18,592	7,840
6	25,403	18,592	6,811
7	24,311	18,592	5,719
8	23,155	18,592	4,563
9	21,928	18,592	3,336
10	20,629	18,592	2,037
11	19,251	18,592	659

[6] Reg. § 1.72-9, Table V.

12	17,790	18,592	- 802
13	16,242	18,592	- 2,350
14	14,601	18,592	- 3,991
15	12,862	18,592	- 5,730
16	11,018	18,592	- 7,574
17	9,064	18,592	- 9,528
18	6,992	18,592	-11,600
19	4,796	18,592	-13,796
20	2,468	18,592	-16,124

[a] Year 1: $500,000 x .06 = $30,000.

The tax deferral benefits from the use of the IRS mandated formula can be substantial. Benefits from this example include:

- Deferred interest for Year 1 [$11,408] is not effectively recaptured until years 12 through 15,

- Deferred interest for Year 2 [$10,592] is not effectively recaptured until years 15 and 16, and

- Deferred interest for Years 3 through 11 [$49,505] is not effectively recaptured until years 17 through 20.

PRACTICE POINTER: Visual presentation of an example, such as the one above, may better allow some clients to grasp the concept of tax deferral, an area that for some may otherwise be too abstract to clearly understand.

TAX PLANNING: Annuities may provide opportunities to significantly reduce income for a short period of time in order to qualify for certain threshold limitations. If, for example, a taxpayer would like to roll over funds from a traditional individual retirement account to a Roth IRA, then an annuity may provide a significant opportunity to reduce income to qualify for the $100,000 AGI threshold, while also providing an accustomed cash flow. Other tax-deferred investments (e.g., exchange-traded funds) may provide opportunities to further reduce threshold income, but may not be as helpful in generating current cash flow.

¶604 An Annuity's Tax Deferral Benefits Can Be Extended through Section 1035 Exchanges

While annuities provide opportunities to defer recognition of income, there is a turnaround point (e.g., Year 12 in the previous example) where the investor will be recognizing more taxable than economic income. Investors may, however, extend and/or increase the deferral benefit by exchanging an existing annuity for a new annuity. An additional benefit, for some investors is that the new annuity does not have to be a life annuity.[7]

---

[7] Per Rev. Rul. 92-95 (1992-2 CB 43), a life annuity exchanged for an annuity of a fixed term qualified for Section 1035 exchange treatment.

Example 2: The investor in the previous example exchanges the annuity after a holding period of 11 years for a new life annuity, also earning 6 percent per year.

Actuarial (economic) value=$296,505

Tax basis=$225,000[a]

Life=12 years[b]

Annual payment=$35,366

Exclusion=$18,750[c]

Year	Compound Interest Earned	Current Year Reportable Interest	Tax Deferred Interest
1 (12)	$17,790	$16,616	$ 1,174
2 (13)	16,736	16,616	120
3 (14)	15,618	16,616	- 998
4 (15)	14,433	16,616	- 2,183
5 (16)	13,177	16,616	- 3,439
6 (17)	11,846	16,616	- 4,770
7 (18)	10,435	16,616	- 6,181
8 (19)	8,939	16,616	- 7,677
9 (20)	7,353	16,616	- 9,263
10 (21)	5,672	16,616	- 10,944
11 (22)	3,891	16,616	- 12,725
12 (23)	2,002	16,616	- 14,614

[a] Basis had been reduced at a rate of $25,000/year for 11 years.
[b] Actual expected life per table is 11.9 years.
[c] $225,000/12 = $18,750.

Benefits from the exchange include:

- Two years of tax deferral (total of 13 years) are added to the original investment,

- A significant amount of interest, $38,283 is deferred to the three years that are added to the original life of the annuity,

- If the taxpayer lives past 85, the higher income may be recognized at a time when he is more likely to be in a lower marginal tax bracket (e.g., no part-time employment), and

- If taxpayer dies prior to expiration of the expected life cycle, he has benefited from having a disproportionate portion of basis absorbed, allowing a disproportionately high deferral of income.

.01 Partial Exchanges of Annuities May Qualify for Tax-Free Status

Partial transfers of annuities to purchase new annuities from unrelated insurance companies may qualify for tax-free status, according to Rev. Ruling 2003-76. The ruling described a scenario where a taxpayer made a direct transfer of 60 percent of the cash surrender value of an annuity contract in exchange for a new annuity contract from an unrelated insurance company. The Service indicated that such a transaction would qualify as a tax-free exchange, but also advised that the provisions of Notice 2003-51 are still applicable. In that notice, the Service indicated that they are considering whether to presumptively conclude, where a partial exchange is followed by a surrender or distribution within 24 months, that such an exchange was made for tax avoidance purposes. The notice also indicated, however, that the Service is also considering whether to treat any distribution that would not be subject to the 10 percent penalty tax imposed under section 72(q) (e.g., distribution after age 59 1/2), as successfully rebutting that presumption.

> **PRACTICE POINTER:** A significant benefit from a Section 1035 exchange may be the opportunity to shift out of an annuity charging high fees (e.g., operating expenses and life insurance) to one with lower costs. While the average annual expense for variable annuities has exceeded two percent, there has been a sea change in the industry. Investors may now find it possible to purchase a variety of annuities from highly rated insurance companies for fees of one percent or less. Also, such policies may often be purchased without incurring potentially high early surrender fees.

> **PRACTICE POINTER:** Practitioners may aid their clients by reviewing the terms and surrender charges of existing annuities. If an investor is holding a fixed annuity and market rates have risen since the time of the annuity's issuance, it may make sense to recommend a Section 1035 exchange in cases where there are no or minimal surrender charges. Typically surrender charges are highest initially (e.g., seven percent in the 1st year) and decrease gradually (e.g., one percent in the 7th year).

.02 General Rule and Simplified Method for Calculating Life Expectancies

In general, exclusions for qualified employee plans and/or tax-sheltered annuities[8] with starting dates after November 18, 1996 must be computed using the "Simplified Method."[9] Other individuals, purchasers of private and/or commercial annuities, must use the "General Rule."

The actuarial tables for the simplified method provide expected returns that in most age brackets are roughly equivalent to the amount provided in the general rule. An individual with a starting date of age 62, for example, would have an expected return multiple of 270 months under the general rule and 260 month under the simplified rule.

Older employees who have the opportunity to participate in their company's qualified annuity plan should evaluate whether they would be better served by participating in that plan or, instead, purchasing a commercial annuity.

In general, the objective will be to use the table with the shortest life expectancy in order to maximize the annual exclusion.

---

[8] Tax-sheltered annuities are special annuity plans or contracts purchased by public schools or tax-exempt organizations for their employees.

[9] Individuals who, at the annuity starting date, are age 75 or older and are entitled to five or more years of guaranteed payments are not required to use the Simplified Method (Code Sec. 72(d)(1)(E)).

Example 3: Abraham is considering participating in his employer's qualified annuity plan, with a starting date of age 70. If he participates in the plan he will be required to use the simplified method" and use an expected return of 210 months. Alternatively, if he were to purchase a commercial annuity, he would be required to employ the" general method" and use an expected return of 192 months. The general method, therefore, would provide the greater opportunity to defer income, because a greater portion would be excluded in early years.

If Abraham were to die prior to recovering his full basis in the investment, a deduction for the remaining amount would be allowed on the decedent's final return.[10] Alternatively, if payments were to continue after the full basis had been recovered, then they would be includable in taxable income.[11]

PRACTICE POINTER: In comparing the benefits of participating in a qualified plan or purchasing a commercial annuity, consideration should be given to costs, which often favor the qualified plan, and range of choices, where private purchases may provide greater flexibility.

¶605 Private Annuities Can Reduce Expenses and Provide Estate Planning Benefits

Individuals in some cases may avoid the expenses associated with company issued annuities by entering into private annuity transactions. A typical annuity transaction would involve a parent transferring property to a child in exchange for an unsecured promise of annuity payments. Normally, where there is a transfer of appreciated property, it is important that the promise be unsecured in order to avoid immediate recognition of gain.[12] In order to avoid being subject to transfer taxes, the value of the property transferred must not be greater than its value as computed under Code Sec. 7520.

.01 Private Annuities, Unlike Sales, May Avoid Application of Related Party Loss Disallowance Rules

Private annuities, unlike sales transactions, may allow for deductions for certain related party transactions. The Service determined that where a woman had entered into private annuities with her four children, the transactions were not governed by Code Sec. 267(a), which generally, disallows losses between related parties. Upon her death, her husband was able to claim a deduction for her unrecovered basis as an itemized deduction.[13]

.02 Private Annuities Can Provide Opportunities for Transferring Appreciated Property

Private annuities can be an effective estate planning tool for transferring appreciated property, particularly where an individual is in poor health and appears unlikely to live as long as the duration contained in the applicable life

---

[10] Code Sec. 72(b)(3).   [12] *Estate of Lloyd G. Bell*, 60 T.C. 469 (1973).

[11] Code Sec. 72(b)(2).   [13] Field Service Advice 1998-462.

expectancy table. If, however, the individual has less than a 50 percent chance of living for one year then the actuarial tables cannot be used.[14]

> **PRACTICE POINTER:** Discussion of likelihood of death and implementation of related estate planning strategies may depend on the attitude of the client. While some clients may view assessing probability of death as crass and/or morbid, others may welcome the opportunity to potentially increase the amount available to their heirs.

¶606 Annuities May Provide Opportunities to Protect Assets from Creditors and/or Medicaid

.01 Asset Protection from Creditors

Opportunities to protect assets from creditors through annuity investments may be available under federal and/or state law. These opportunities are available because annuities are generally considered insurance products, items that often qualify for special protective status. Although a detailed discussion of the application of the laws governing asset protection status of annuities is not within the scope of this text, advisers should be aware that there may be significant differences between states in the opportunities afforded to protect assets through these vehicles. Further, advisers should be aware that there may also be significant differences even in how states determine what actually qualifies as an annuity.[15]

> **PLANNING POINTER:** If a taxpayer waits until he is under direct threat of litigation, he could potentially lose the protection otherwise afforded by an annuity. Florida law, for example, may deny protected status for an annuity that has been converted from other assets within the past four years if there was an attempt to hinder or delay a creditor.[16] Taxpayers in litigious professions or businesses, therefore, may find it beneficial to invest some holdings in annuities even in cases where there would be some loss in investment return or liquidity.

.02 Offshore Annuities

Offshore annuities may provide some protection from creditors by making recoveries of assets a costly and difficult process. Annuity contracts offered by the Isle of Man Assurance Ltd., for example, provide that all claims by a policyholder's creditors can only be made through courts within that country, which is located off the coast of England.[17]

---

[14] Reg. § 25.7520-3(b)(3).

[15] *See, for example,* "Hidden in Plain View: The Pension Shield Against Creditors," by Patricia E. Dilley, *Indiana Law Journal,* Spring 1999. For a review by individual states of the protections afforded to life insurance and annuity proceeds, *see also* "Creditor Protection for Life Insurance and Annuities," by Gideon Rothschild and Daniel S. Rubin at www.mosessinger.com/resources/creditprotect.shtml.

[16] Fla. Stat. Ann. Sec. 222.30.

[17] "Offshore Annuities Give the Benefit of Privacy," by Bridget O'Brien, *Dow Jones Online News,* January 26, 1998.

PRACTICE POINTER: Investors who are considering investing in an offshore annuity should be advised that such investments, which are not marketed in the U.S., are not subject to S.E.C. protection.

.03 Medicaid Protection

Annuities in some cases may allow some individuals to qualify for Medicaid without depleting all or virtually all of their assets. Annuities may be particularly helpful in cases of married couples where one spouse is healthy and the other requires the services of a nursing home. In general, where one spouse enters a nursing home, the other spouse may keep up to half of their total assets to a maximum of $87,000 (in 2001) and a house and a car, without causing a disqualification for Medicaid. If, however, the excess money is converted into an annuity for the healthier spouse, it may remove the availability of assets beyond the threshold maximum.[18] Opportunities to protect assets may also be available for single individuals through vehicles such as an annuity with a balloon payment.

PRACTICE POINTER: The timing for the beginning of annuity payments may be critical for the determination of whether an individual will qualify for Medicaid benefits. In some cases, if an individual applies for Medicaid benefits before annuitization begins, he will be required to cash in or pay down the annuity to recover excessive assets.[19]

PRACTICE POINTER: The rules governing qualification for Medicaid benefits are complicated and vary by state. Consequences of erroneous or incomplete advice can be potentially devastating (e.g., improper timing of annuitization can cause an individual to be disqualified for benefits). Further, many state programs conduct investigations to search for illegal and/or abusive practices. Practitioners, therefore, who are not specialists in this area may want to seriously consider consulting with a professional who does specialize in this area before developing any plan that includes as objectives the protection of assets and qualification for Medicaid benefits.

---

[18] "Suddenly Poor: Insurers Help Elderly Get Medicaid to Pay for Nursing Homes–Annuity that Converts Assets Into Income Can Let Even Affluent People Qualify–States Start to Crack Down," by Ann Davis, *The Wall Street Journal*, June 6, 2001.

[19] "Mine Fields with Annuities and Medicaid," by Tyrone M. Clark, *National Underwriter/Life & Health Financial Services*, June 1, 1998, Vol. 102, Issue 22, p. 13.

Chapter 7

CHARITABLE CONTRIBUTIONS

¶701 Donations of Appreciated Property May Allow for Exclusion of Capital Gains

Contributions of property that would meet the criteria for recognition as long-term capital gains may, subject to certain restrictions, be deducted in full (i.e., current fair market value) without recognition of taxable income. The use of contributions of appreciated property can provide a very simple and practical means of avoiding the recognition of capital gains, while still allowing a full charitable donation. The benefit for donating appreciated capital gain property is, however, limited to thirty percent of adjusted gross income per year. Excess amounts, as is the case with excess contributions of cash, may be carried forward for five years.

> **TAX PLANNING:** Contributions of appreciated property may be particularly beneficial for donors who are residents of states with high tax rates that base their assessments on federal taxation. A taxpayer who resides in such states, therefore, can receive an overall benefit for contributions significantly in excess of the maximum 20 percent federal rate.

In some unusual cases, for example, the application of California's alternative minimum tax, the untaxed federal gain may be subject to gain recognition.[1]

> **PRACTICE POINTER:** Practitioners can aid their clients who make regular charitable contributions (e.g., annual contribution to a religious organization) by identifying and suggesting appreciated stocks and bonds for contribution. The client should be advised that even if she does not wish to divest herself of an investment she still can benefit from a step-up in basis.

> **Example 1:** Sharon Silver, a financial adviser to Sue, finds that she is holding $5,000 in XYZ stock that had been purchased a number of years ago for $1,000. Sharon is also aware that Sue normally contributes $5,000 to a local religious organization. Sue has been happy with the performance of XYZ stock and does not want to divest herself of that holding.

> Sue can maintain her holdings in XYZ stock and obtain the benefits of a $5,000 charitable deduction and a step-up in basis for her XYZ stock from $1,000 to $5,000 through the following actions:

> 1. Donate the original XYZ stock to the charitable organization, and

> 2. Immediately purchase replacement shares of XYZ stock.

---

[1] California never changed its law to reflect the change in the federal alternative minimum tax, where unrecognized appreciation was removed as a tax preference item.

Sue is able to achieve these benefits because the "wash sale" provisions, requiring deferral of losses where substantially identical property is replaced within thirty days before or after the transaction, do not apply to transactions where the property disposed of would result in a gain.

.01 Exceptions and Limitations

An individual is not entitled to the exclusion of long-term capital gains for the following donations of appreciated property:

- Gifts of other than "qualified appreciated stock[2]" to certain private nonoperating foundations,[3]

- Tangible personal property unrelated to the charity's business or function[4], and

- Property for which the taxpayer elects to disregard the 30 percent limitation that normally applies for charitable contributions of property.

PRACTICE POINTER: In order to claim a charitable contribution for stock in excess of basis, the shareholder must be able to substantiate that shares are "qualified appreciated stock" under Code Sec. 170 (e)(5)(B). Shares may not qualify, for example, in cases where there are no market quotations on an established securities market on the day of transfer.[5]

.02 Appraisal Requirement for Property Valued in Excess of $5,000

In general, except for contributions of public traded securities, appraisals must be obtained from qualified appraisers for donations of property in excess of $5,000. For contributions of art with an appraised value of $20,000 or more, a photograph must be attached to the taxpayer's return.

PRACTICE POINTER: In cases where a qualified appraisal is required, taxpayers should be certain to obtain it from an individual who meets standards as a qualified appraiser. In *D'Arcangelo*,[6] a taxpayer's claim for a $40,000 charitable deduction for artwork and art supplies was totally denied, largely because the person who made the appraisal, an employee of the charitable beneficiary, was not a qualified "appraiser" within the meaning of Reg. § 1.170A-13.

¶702 Charitable Bequests of U.S. Savings Bonds May Benefit Charities at Low After-Tax Cost

Lifetime transfers of savings bonds to qualified charitable organizations generally provide no tax benefits beyond that afforded by cash contributions, and have the detriment of requiring recognition in the current year of all accrued interest. Testamentary charitable bequests of savings bonds, however, can potentially provide significant income and estate tax benefits.

---

[2] Stock that is publicly traded and would qualify for capital gains treatment (Code Sec. 170(e)(5)(B).

[3] Code Sec. 170(e)(1)(B)(ii).

[4] Code Sec. 170(e)(1)(B)(i).

[5] John C. Todd, 118 TC No. 19 (2002).

[6] T.C. Memo 1994-572 (1994).

Normally, savings bond interest is treated as income in respect of a decedent (i.e., income that has been earned by a taxpayer but has not been included because of a taxpayer's accounting method). Such income, absent a qualifying charitable bequest, is taxable as a property interest included in the taxable estate[7] and, depending on the executor's actions, as either:

1. Income includable on the decedent's final return,
2. Income taxable to the estate, or
3. Income taxable to the beneficiary.

An estate or its beneficiary may, however, avoid recognition of U.S. savings bonds interest by specifically bequeathing it to a charitable organization. A specific bequest would have the effect of transferring recognition of income to the recipient. If the recipient is a charitable organization, normally no tax would result.[8] IRS Letter Ruling 9845026 describes three key factors that allow for this favorable treatment:

1. Reg. § 1.661(a)-2(f): provides, in part, that where property is distributed in kind, no gain or loss is to be recognized by the estate unless the distribution is in satisfaction of a right to a specific dollar amount or specific property other than that distributed.
2. Reg. § 1.691(a)-4(b)(2): provides, in part, that where a right of income is transferred to a residuary legatee, only that person must report it in gross income.
3. Reg. § 501(c)(3): provides that an organization that qualifies as an exempt organization will not be subject to income tax.

TAX PLANNING: Other attractive items for charitable bequests, based on the reasoning of the above letter ruling, would include traditional individual retirement accounts, qualified plan benefits,[9] sole proprietor's accounts receivable, and unpaid compensation.

PRACTICE POINTER: It may be beneficial to have wills provide that charitable bequests should first be satisfied by IRD items and, only after those items have been exhausted, to use other assets of the estate. Specific bequests of such items to specific charities may help ensure that the transfers will be in accordance with compliance requirements.[10]

¶703 Donor-Advised Funds Provide Tax and Flexibility Benefits for Donations of Appreciated Investments

While some investors may find the opportunity to donate appreciated stock without incurring capital gains an attractive option, others may find it to be a cumbersome process, lacking in flexibility. The use of a donor-advised fund, however, can provide simple cost-effective means for individuals to obtain

---

[7] Code Sec. 2033.

[8] Private foundations may, however, be subject to a 2 percent excise tax on interest income (Code Sec. 4940).

[9] Spousal consent is normally required to designate a beneficiary other than the decedent's spouse.

[10] Code Sec. 642(c) provides that income must be distributed pursuant to the governing instrument's terms.

benefits for the donation of appreciated stocks and securities. A donor-advised fund serves as an intermediary for the collection of charitable donations.

Example 2: Matt Brady is a broker whose income is subject to substantial yearly fluctuations. In addition, his investment portfolio typically incurs significant volatility. Despite these uncertainties, Matt's preferences are to:

1. Claim larger deductions for charitable contributions in those years when his marginal tax rate is high, while

2. Maintaining relatively consistent payments to a local religious organization and other charitable groups.

Matt, without the use of donor-advised fund or other intermediary, may find it difficult to receive the optimal benefits for donations of appreciated property while also meeting his goals for charitable giving. In some years he would make donations while at a lower marginal tax bracket and/or when there is little available appreciated stock. In other years he would have appreciated stock in excess of the amount he wishes to donate.

The use of a donor-advised fund would allow Matt to compensate for the volatility in his income by allowing him to make donations to a charitable fund at a time that is optimal for tax and investing purposes, while delaying actual payments to the charitable organizations until the desired period. In most cases, the donor simply has to direct the fund to make a specific charitable contribution from his account.

Major brokerage institutions (e.g., Fidelity, Schwab, and Vanguard),[11] allow donors to open accounts to their charitable gift funds with donations of as little as $10,000. Even for larger donors, however, the benefits of these accounts may be attractive as compared to establishing and operating a private foundation. These benefits include:

- No required annual distributions [Private foundations must distribute a fixed percentage annually],

- Donors are allowed to deduct up to 30 percent of AGI for contributions of appreciated property [Donations for private foundations are limited to 20 percent],

- Greater privacy [Private foundations are required to make public copies of their records], and

- Avoidance of professional fees for drafting documents and filing tax returns [Private foundations are required to prepare annual reports].

PRACTICE POINTER: Donor-advised funds may be useful for year-end rebalancing of portfolio assets. Individuals who would be forced to recognize gains because of their desire to rebalance their portfolio can avoid recognition of gains, but still defer donations to actual charitable organizations until a time of their choice.

---

[11] Names are provided only for purposes of description, not necessarily endorsement.

.01 Specialized Donor-Advised Funds for Real Estate and Other Illiquid Assets

Individuals who are interested in donating appreciated real estate may often find that charities are reluctant or unwilling to accept the donation because, at least, of a perception of potential problems of liquidity, valuation, and liability.[12] Specialized donor-advised funds may be available, however, for donations of real estate and other illiquid assets.

> **PRACTICE POINTER:** Donations of appreciated real estate to charities that are not well equipped to handle them may result in a reduction of the amount allowable as charitable donations. Alternatively, contributions to funds that specialize in real estate may allow contributors the best opportunity to receive the full value of the donated property, while still providing the proceeds to the charity of their choice.

In practice, many charities may be reluctant to recommend the utilization of an intermediary, such as a specialized donor-advised fund, because after the donation is made to the fund, the donor still maintains the right to designate that the proceeds be used for charities other than their own.[13] A fund-raiser may prefer a "bird-in-hand," even if it means that the amount of proceeds ultimately received is somewhat lower than could be achieved through the usage of a specialized DAF.

¶704 Charitable Gift Annuities Provide Current Charitable Deductions and Deferred Capital Gain Recognition

Another potentially attractive way to contribute appreciated property is through a charitable gift annuity. A typical charitable gift annuity provides that a charitable organization, in exchange for cash or property, will distribute a fixed sum of cash to a donor annually for each remaining year of his life. The amount of the annual payment, normally lower than that for a commercial annuity, will vary depending upon prevailing interest rates and the age of the donor.

The donor of appreciated property to a charity through a charitable gift annuity receives tax benefits in two ways. First, the donor receives a charitable donation for the amount by which the present value of the contributed property exceeds the value of the life annuity. Second, recognition of both ordinary and capital gain is deferred in accordance with the rules for reporting of proceeds from an annuity under Section 72. These provisions allow a portion of each payment to be treated as a return of capital. Also, since these rules are based on simple, rather than compound income factors, they allow for less income to be recognized in early years than would under a method reflecting true economic growth.[14] A detriment of contributing appreciated property through an annuity, rather than outright or through a donor-advised fund is that the capital gain must be recognized, albeit, on a deferred basis.

---

[12] These issues are discussed in more detail in "The Donor-Advised Fund: A Flexible Vehicle for Real Estate Gifts," in *"Fund Raising Management,"* by Ethel Kaplan, July 2000, Vol. 31, Issue 5, pp. 8-10.

[13] *Ibid.*

[14] *See* Chapter 6 for a fuller discussion of the tax deferral benefits of annuities.

The amount of the annual payments is determined, in most cases, in accordance with rates established by The American Council on Gift Annuities. Rates are based on the following assumptions:

- 50 percent residuum (amount of original contribution remaining at death),
- Usage of female life expectancies,
- Annual administrative costs of 75 basis points, and
- Portfolio of 30 percent equities, 60 percent 10-year Treasury bonds and 10 percent cash equivalents.[15]

The single life rates, approved by the American Council on Gift Annuities, effective July 1, 2003, for an individual 65 years old is 6.0 percent, per year. The rate for an 85-year-old is 9.5 percent.

PRACTICE POINTER: Although the Council bases its rates on a relatively conservative portfolio (e.g., 60 percent 10-year Treasury bonds), charities may invest more aggressively, potentially increasing the long-term risk for a donor. The fact that in most cases the charity's promise to pay annuity payments is not limited to its usage of investment assets may often not provide significant additional protection, because there may be little other liquid assets available. Therefore, a donor considering entering into a charitable gift annuity should carefully evaluate the charity's investing policies prior to entering into an agreement that can extend for an extended number of years.

PRACTICE POINTER: Many potential donors may not be aware of the opportunities to contribute to charitable gift annuities. Gift annuities normally may not be sold by brokers, agents, or others on a commission basis. Under the Philanthropy Protection Act of 1995, charitable gift annuities and charitable remainder trusts are made exempt from regulation by the Securities and Exchange Commission, provided that commissions are not paid to solicitors for their sale.

TAX PLANNING: A potentially ideal time for a contribution through a charitable gift annuity is in a taxpayer's final year of work prior to retirement. A taxpayer would receive a charitable contribution while in a high tax bracket, but would be recognizing income during retirement years, when she is likely to be in a lower tax bracket. If the taxpayer cannot use all of the charitable deduction in the current year, then it may be more beneficial to make the contribution earlier and allow carryforwards to be used while the taxpayer is still in a high marginal tax bracket. Carryforwards are limited to the five years immediately following the donation.

Other potentially beneficial times for contributions include: 1) a taxpayer is in an unusually high tax bracket as a result of a bonus, investments, etc.; and 2) taxpayer would like to qualify to meet a threshold requirement (e.g., Roth IRA rollover or Hope Education Credit).

---

[15] American Council on Gift Annuities, discussion of rates effective July 1, 2003. www.acga-web.org.

¶705 Charitable Remainder Trusts—Potentially Significant Benefits, but Limited Practical Applications

Charitable remainder trusts potentially provide a significant tax benefit beyond that offered by charitable gift annuities. In addition to providing a current benefit for charitable contributions and reducing the taxable estate, charitable remainder trusts also provide the benefit of full exclusion of gain on the contribution. Charitable gift annuities, by comparison, require recognition of capital gain during the payout period. The amount of the allowable charitable contribution is determined in a manner similar to that of the charitable gift trust (i.e., consideration of donor's age, value of the retained interest, and government's current interest rate assumption).

A typical charitable reminder trust transaction involves a contribution of a highly appreciated asset to a trust and annual cash payouts to the donor. The trustee of the trust can sell the asset without recognition of capital gain. Common reasons for selling the contributed asset include increasing the trust's liquidity and portfolio diversification.

Two forms of charitable remainder trusts are basically available for preferred tax treatment:

1. Charitable remainder annuity trust (CRAT), and

2. Charitable remainder unit trust (CRUT).

The noncharitable beneficiary of a CRAT generally receives fixed annuity payments, while the beneficiary of a CRUT receives income that is a fixed percentage of the trust's net assets. The beneficiary of a CRUT, therefore, will receive a varying stream of income, assuming there are variations in the annual net asset values of the trust.

> **PRACTICE POINTER:** An additional benefit for donors of a CRT is that its trustee may invest the proceeds more conservatively than would a trustee of a fund investing charitable gift annuity donations. This may be an important consideration where the period of payout is likely to be for an extended period of time (e.g., thirty years or more).

.01 Complexities of Drafting and Administration May Limit Viability of CRTs

Despite their potential benefits, the complexity related costs for compliance and administration of CRTs may make them practical only for relatively large straight-forward contributions of highly appreciated property. While the IRS does provide "safe-harbor" sample trust forms under Rev. Procs. 89-20,[16] 89-21,[17] 90-30,[18] 90-31,[19] and 90-32,[20] not all taxpayers' needs may be addressed by them. Drafting issues not addressed in the forms may arise, for example, regarding a trustee's power to allocate ("sprinkle"), income to beneficiaries. Other drafting

---

[16] Rev. Proc. 89-20, 1989-1 CB 841.
[17] Rev. Proc. 89-21, 1989-1 CB 842.
[18] Rev. Proc. 90-30, 1990-1 CB 534.
[19] Rev. Proc. 90-31, 1990-1 CB 539.
[20] Rev. Proc. 90-32, 1990-1 CB 546.

issues may include structuring the power of the trustee to delay payment. While Code Sec. 674(b)(6) permits trustees the power to delay payment, such right is forbidden under Rev. Rul. 72-395.[21]

Administrative complexities may also reduce the attractiveness of CRTs. In *Atkinson*,[22] for example, an estate was denied a deduction for the charitable remainder portion of a trust that was intended to be a charitable remainder annuity trust because, in part, certain required minimum payments were not made to the noncharitable beneficiary during her lifetime. An argument presented by the petitioner, that the failure to distribute payments to the beneficiary did not harm the charity, was not deemed valid. A second reason for disallowance of charitable remainder trust treatment was that the trustee planned to invade the CRAT to cover a shortfall in the payment of estate taxes. As a result of the disallowance the trust incurred a very substantial estate tax deficiency.

> **PRACTICE POINTER:** Charitable remainder trusts, in order to be beneficial, should provide tax benefits that will outweigh the costs and potential risks associated with their drafting and administration. If a client's needs can be served by the IRS provided sample trust forms and administrative costs are below that of the CRT's benefits, then such a transaction may make sense. Clients should be aware, however, that an error in drafting and/or compliance could result in severe consequences. Practitioners should be aware that such errors could potentially lead to significant client claims of malpractice.

¶706 Charitable Lead Trusts (CLTs) May Provide Significant Transfer Tax Benefits for Seriously, but Not Terminally, Ill Taxpayers

Although the establishment of a charitable lead trust (CLT) during an individual's lifetime is often not as beneficial as that of a charitable remainder trust, such creation can potentially provide significant transfer tax benefits for an individual who is seriously, but not terminally, ill. In cases where there is a reasonable expectation that an individual or certain qualified family members will not live as long as the table amount, but will live at least 12-18 months (discussed below), a tax savings may arise because the remainder interest, subject to gift tax, will be valued at a rate based on average life expectancies, rather than on the shorter anticipated life expectancy.

Charitable lead trusts, conceptually, are the opposite of a charitable remainder trust. Whereas a charitable remainder trust provides that gift beneficiaries receive an income interest and a charitable organization receives the remainder, a charitable lead trust provides that the charitable organization receives an income interest and the gift beneficiaries receive the remainder.

---

[21] These and other issues of drafting and compliance are discussed in "Charitable Remainder Trusts: An Overview," by Paul D. Callister, *The Tax Lawyer*, Spring 1998, Vol. 51, pp. 549-571.

[22] 115 T.C. 26 (2000).

The detriments to creating charitable lead trusts during an individual's lifetime can be substantial and, except for certain unusual situations such as the one discussed here (i.e., transfers by a seriously but not terminally ill individual), generally results in such trusts being a less favored tool for estate planning than other means. These detriments include:

1. **Transfers do not qualify as charitable donations.** Additionally the income generated by a CLT, not structured as a grantor trust, can potentially be taxable to the entity. The CLT may escape income taxation, generally, only where the charitable contributions of the CLT exceed the amount of income earned.

   TAX PLANNING: Although a donor, theoretically, could obtain an income tax deduction for payments to the charitable organization by structuring the CLT as a grantor trust, such action would generally be inadvisable because the donor would be taxed on the trust's income.

   TAX PLANNING: Creation of a CLT could prove to be counterproductive in the event that a donor dies in a year that the estate tax repeal is in effect (e.g., 2010 or, should the estate tax repeal be extended or made permanent, a later year). If such a case arose, the donor would likely have benefited more had he made a direct contribution to the charitable organization, allowing him to claim a currently deductible charitable donation.

2. **Gifts to a CLT do not qualify for the annual gift tax exclusion.** The importance of this factor may vary depending upon whether a) intended beneficiaries are already receiving gifts equal to the annual exclusion and/or b) the donor has fully utilized the amount available for transfer under the unified credit.

3. **Application of the generation-skipping tax may create complications for planning for transfers to "skip persons," particularly after the Economic Growth and Reconciliation Act of 2001 (EGTRRA).**[23] One concern is the determination of a GST inclusion ratio for a charitable lead annuity trust (trust provides for a fixed payment each year). This amount cannot be determined until after the charitable term has ended. If after the term had ended, the value of the trust has increased, an otherwise hoped for outcome, a portion of the value of that trust could be subject to the GST.[24]

.01 Individuals Qualified for CLT Life Measurement

In order for an individual to qualify for use of the IRS average life expectancy tables, contained in Reg. § 20.2031-7, the following requirements must be met:

---

[23] Detailed discussion of the generation-skipping tax is beyond the scope of this text. For more information see "Generation-Skipping Transfer Tax Planning after the 2001 Act: Mostly Good News," by Carol A. Harrington, Carlyn S. McCaffrey, Lloyd Leva Plaine, and Pam H. Schneider, *The Journal of Taxation*, Volume 95, September 2001.

[24] Charitable lead unitrusts, alternatively, provide for fixed percentage payments based on net worth and, therefore, allow for the allocation of the GST amount at the creation of the CLT, rather than at the termination of the charitable interest.

1. The individual who is used for the life expectancy tables must be either:

   a. the donor

   b. the donor's spouse

   c. an individual who, with respect to all noncharitable beneficiaries, is either 1) a linear ancestor or 2) the spouse of a linear ancestor of those beneficiaries

2. The remainder beneficiaries, as related to the individual used for life expectancy tables, must be lineal descendents and can include the lineal step-relatives (e.g., step-children).

Exception. This requirement is satisfied, even where non-lineal beneficiaries potentially may receive the remainder interest, in cases where there is a less than 15 percent probability that such an event will occur.

> **Example 3:** A charitable lead annuity trust provides for the annuity to be paid to a charity for the life of Alice who is age 75, on the date the annuity is created. The trust instrument provides that on Alice's death, the corpus is to pass to Alice's only child, Bonnie, who is age 50, on the date of the annuity's creation. The trust also provides that if Bonnie predeceases Alice, the remainder is to go to Bonnie's children. If, however, as is the case at the time of the CLAT's creation, Bonnie has no living children, the remainder is to go to Alice's heirs at law, including nonlineal family members such as siblings and aunts and uncles. A computation, based on the currently applicable Life Table contained in Reg. § 20.2031-7 indicates that there is a 10.462 percent probability that Bonnie will predecease her mother and, therefore, under such circumstances the remainder interest would pass to nonlineal descendents. Since the likelihood of this event is less than 15 percent, the CLAT will meet the requirements that all noncharitable beneficiaries be lineal descendents.[25]

3. The individual must not be terminally ill at the time of the transaction.

An individual is considered to be terminally ill in cases where he is deemed to have at least a fifty percent probability of dying within one year after the transfer. An individual who survives for at least 18 months after the transaction is presumed not to have been terminally ill, "unless the contrary is established by clear and convincing evidence."[26]

> **PRACTICE POINTER:** Clients who are considering using CLTs, for purposes of benefiting from average life tables, should be reminded that survival of an illness for at least 18 months beyond the transaction point, provides a presumption, but not a guarantee, that such illness will be treated as having been nonterminal.

> **PRACTICE POINTER:** Concerns may arise regarding the propriety and ethics of establishing a plan that, to be successful, essentially requires the

---

[25] Example is adapted from the one contained in the supplementary background information section of TD RIN 1545-AX74, "Lifetime Charitable Lead Trusts," 66 FR 1040, Treas. Dec. Int. Rev. 8923.

[26] Reg. § 20.7520-3(b)(3).

premature death of the taxpayer or other related individual. For some clients, even raising the issue of developing a plan based on such a premise, may be viewed as improper. Other clients, however, under the circumstances, may welcome the opportunity to maximize the amount of wealth they can transfer to charities and beneficiaries, while reducing the amount to be transferred to the government.

Case law has established the validity of utilizing official valuation tables, based on averages, in cases where such tables may produce distorted results. In *Estate of McLendon,* for example, the Court ruled: "Where the Commissioner has specifically approved a valuation methodology, like actuarial tables, in its own revenue ruling, he will not be heard to fault a taxpayer for taking advantage of the tax minimization opportunities inherent therein."[27]

TAX PLANNING: If there is a reasonable likelihood that the individual may live until 2010 or later, the following factors should be considered before establishing a CLT:

1. If the taxpayer dies in a year in which the estate tax is not in effect, the taxpayer will have made a transfer for which he has received no tax benefit and has lost the opportunity to receive one (e.g., current charitable donation for a direct transfer of property).

2. Amounts actually paid for gift taxes on the creation of a CLT are not refundable in the event that the estate tax is repealed. Taxpayers may, therefore, want to consider limiting the amount of the gift component of the CLT so as to not exceed the amount allowable for tax-free gifts under the existing uniform transfer tax schedule.

.02 Other Potential Uses for a Charitable Lead Trust

Although, as mentioned previously, CLTs have a number of significant inherent detriments, there may be special circumstances, in addition to the situation of a potentially life-shortening illness, where its establishment may be beneficial. Such situations may include:

1. **A taxpayer who would like to make additional charitable donations, but has exhausted all current and future allowances (i.e., carryovers) for charitable donations.** Where further direct contributions of charity would provide no income tax deduction, a contribution through a CLT could potentially produce at least some transfer tax benefits.

2. **A charitably inclined taxpayer would like to delay the time at which a beneficiary would receive assets.** Such situations could arise, for example, where a taxpayer is concerned that his adult child is not in a stable marriage and/or not mature enough to manage significant sums of money.

---

[27] *Estate of McLendon,* 135 F.3d 1017 (CA-5, 1998), rev'g TCM 1996-307. *See also Ithaca Trust Co.,* 279 U.S. 151, 155 (2. Ct., 1929). These cases are discussed in more detail in "New Regulations Sanction Accelerated Charitable Lead Trusts," by Randall D. Van Dolson, *Estate Planning,* Vol. 28, April 2001.

Chapter 8

COLLEGE FUNDING

¶801 Roth IRAs—Often the Best Starting Point for Eligible Individuals

Individuals who are eligible to contribute to Roth IRAs may find them to be the ideal starting point for investing for a dependent's education. The Roth IRA provides the investor with the opportunity to generate tax-exempt income and maintain a high level of flexibility without significantly reducing opportunities for family members to obtain financial aid.

The advantages in flexibility are twofold. First, the funds contained in a Roth IRA do not necessarily have to be used for any particular individual's education. If, for example, an intended child receives a full scholarship or, perhaps, decides not to attend college, the parent can continue to indefinitely hold the funds in the retirement account or, alternatively, withdraw it in accordance with the liberal distribution rules applicable to IRAs. Second, unlike Section 529 plans, discussed in ¶803, which significantly reduce an individual's opportunities to manage investments, Roth IRAs allow the investor to directly choose their investment holdings.

Holding college savings in an IRA can also provide important benefits in maintaining a family's eligibility for financial aid because in most cases they are treated as a retirement asset and, therefore, not considered as a potential source of college funding.

> **PRACTICE POINTER:** Families planning for college should be aware, however, that some private colleges are beginning to place limits on the amount that is exempt.[1] Also, colleges, in response to the asset shifting strategies of families, could potentially adjust their own guidelines and begin to require that Roth IRA contributions be considered as a source of college funding.

Benefits of Roth IRAs for college funding include:

1. **Contributions can be withdrawn tax-free.** These amounts, following passage of the Economic Growth and Tax Relief Reconciliation Act, can be substantial, even for younger taxpayers who do not qualify for the Roth "catch-up" provisions.

    Example 1: Harry and Harriet Hathaway, each age 35, in 2004 begin contributing the maximum allowable to their Roth IRA accounts. After ten years they would have $90,000 available for college funding, assuming there

---

[1] As reported in "10 Things Your College Won't Tell You," smartmoney.com/college/finaid.

was not a net loss in the value of the investments. Their maximum allowable contribution amounts are shown below.

Year	Maximum	Allowable Contribution
2004	$6,000	[$3,000/taxpayer]
2005	$8,000	[$4,000/taxpayer]
2006	$8,000	[$4,000/taxpayer]
2007	$8,000	[$4,000/taxpayer]
2008	$10,000	[$5,000/taxpayer]
2009	$10,000	[$5,000/taxpayer]
2010	$10,000	[$5,000/taxpayer]
2011	$10,000	[$5,000/taxpayer]
2012	$10,000	[$5,000/taxpayer]
2013	$10,000	[$5,000/taxpayer]
	$90,000	Total

Income amounts may not be withdrawn, without being subject to tax, but will continue to grow for their retirement or other purposes. If funds were withdrawn, however, they would not be subject to the penalty that otherwise applies for distributions made prior to the taxpayer being age 59 1/2.[2]

2. **Increased contributions are allowed, under the Roth "catch-up," provisions for taxpayers who are age 50 or over.** In the previous example, if all of the contributions had been made by parents who met the age qualifications, the total allowable contributions would have increased by $9,000/taxpayer, for total allowable contributions of $108,000.

TAX PLANNING: Individuals who plan on withdrawing contributions from their Roth IRAs for funding a child's education, should consider allocating the more conservative portion of their long-term investments to such accounts. If funds lose value, no capital loss may be claimed. Alternatively, if funds do exceptionally well, the additional appreciation may not provide an immediate benefit, since only contributions are being withdrawn for college funding.

The more risky college-related investments may be more appropriate for other vehicles, such as Coverdell Savings Account. While losses are also not deductible in other tax-exempt accounts, such as the Coverdell Savings Account, taxpayers can more easily take advantage of higher performance by drawing on income, as well as contributions, to pay for qualified education expenses.

3. **Parents who are over age 59 1/2 and have met a five-year holding period may withdraw both income and contributions, without being subject to tax or penalty.**[3] Even parents who will be two or three years shy of meeting that age requirement, at the time their child enters college, may still benefit from this provision.

---

[2] The 10 percent penalty normally applicable for distributions made prior to age 59 1/2 does not apply to withdrawals used for qualifying education expenses. Such qualifying expenses include tuition, books, fees, supplies and equipment, but do not include room and board (Code Sec. 72(t)(2)(E)).

[3] Code Sec. 408A(d)(2).

Example 2: Susan Smith, born June 1, 1960, is age 56 in 2016, the year that her daughter enters college as a freshman. Eligibility for withdrawals of funds is shown below.

Fall semester 2016	Freshman	Roth contributions only
Spring semester 2017	Freshman	Roth contributions only
Fall semester 2017	Sophomore	Roth contributions only
Spring semester 2018	Sophomore	Roth contributions only
Fall semester 2018	Junior	Roth contributions only
Spring semester 2019	Junior	Roth contributions and income [taxpayer will be age 59 1/2, before year end]
Fall semester 2020	Senior	Roth contributions and income
Spring semester 2020	Senior	Roth contributions and income

If Susan were to need additional funds slightly earlier (e.g., Fall semester 2018), she might consider borrowing the money through a tax-deductible short-term home equity loan. If, however, borrowing would be required for an extended period of time, other vehicles such as Coverdell Education Savings Accounts or Section 529 Qualified Tuition Plans could be more advantageous.

.01 Planning to Mitigate Effect of Roth Income Eligibility Restriction

A restriction seriously limiting the availability of the Roth IRA benefits is its income eligibility threshold. While the Economic Growth and Tax Relief Reconciliation Act of 2001 significantly increased the level of allowable annual contributions, it, importantly, did not increase the eligibility amount for adjusted gross income above the existing levels (e.g., $150,000 - $160,000 AGI for married couples filing a joint return). Perhaps equally or more important is that these amounts are not adjusted for inflation.

TAX PLANNING: Individuals who anticipate that their income in future years may exceed the threshold for contributing to a Roth IRA might consider borrowing to maximize their contributions prior to exceeding the income threshold. Such borrowing has the added benefit of generating interest expense that in most cases would be deductible as an itemized deduction.[4]

Example 3: Joe Garrett, age 51, and Joan Garrett, age 45, are saving for the education of their daughter whom they expect will be attending college in ten years. Both are working and contributing the maximum allowed to their employers' 401(k) plan. Although they recognize the tax-exclusion benefits of investing in a Roth IRA, they do not have cash available to make allowable contributions. Their anticipated income for the following four years and allowable Roth contributions are shown below.

---

[4] Code Sec. 265(a), disallowing interest expense incurred for the acquisition or holding of tax-exempt interest, generally applies to municipal bonds and regulated investment companies. Detailed discussions of the deductibility of interest expenses are contained in "The Ability of Individual Taxpayers to Deduct 'Interest' Under Current Law: A Roadmap through the Maze," by Patricia Ann Metzer, *54th N.Y.U. Institute on Taxation*, 1996 and" Simplifying the Interest Deduction for Individual Taxpayers," by Martin J. McMahon Jr., *Tax Notes, Special Supplement*, May 28, 2001, pp. 1371-1413.

Year	Projected AGI	Allowable Roth
2004	$130,000	$6,500
2005	$140,000	$8,500
2006	$150,000	$9,000
2007	$165,000	-0-

Joe and Joan take out a home equity loan, at 7.5 percent interest, in order to fund IRAs with certificates of deposit generating five percent annual interest income. Their combined federal and state marginal tax bracket is 33 1/3 percent. The net effect for the year that funds are borrowed, therefore, is to break even. As a result of borrowing, however, they are able to increase their combined balances in their IRAs by $24,000 in principal, plus the interest that has been earned.

In 2007, the year in which the Garrets become ineligible to contribute to Roth IRAs, they may wish to consider maximizing contributions to Coverdell Education Savings Accounts, which have a higher threshold for eligible contributors (e.g., phaseout range for married couples filing jointly is $190,000 - $220,000). Borrowing, similarly to the method used for funding the Roth IRA, could also prove to be beneficial for the Coverdell accounts.

PRACTICE POINTER: The number of individuals who could benefit from borrowing to fund a Roth IRA could be significant. According to the Treasury Department, only 4 percent of eligible taxpayers maximize their contributions to their employer's 401(k) plans.[5]

¶802 Coverdell Education Savings Accounts—A Second Best Option for Many, First Best for a Few

The principle benefits of a Coverdell Education Savings Account (formerly referred to as Education IRAs), are:

1. Income generated by the account is tax-exempt, and

2. Investors can directly choose investments in the account (e.g., select a specific mutual fund).

Coverdell Education Savings Accounts require, however, that funds must be expended for a qualifying education purpose in order to remain tax-exempt. That restriction along with others, including limitations on the ability to claim the tuition expense deduction and/or education credits, often make a Coverdell Education Savings Account a less desirable investment vehicle than a Roth IRA. In limited situations, however, particularly for individuals who will be withdrawing funds prior to the year of reaching age 59 1/2, Coverdell accounts can provide benefits that are more advantageous than those offered by Roth IRAs.

Investors who can benefit from Coverdell Education Savings Account include:

---

[5] Reported in "Tax Bill Provides More Incentives to Save—Complicated Rules will Test Taxpayers," by Bridget O'Brian and Theo Francis, *Wall Street Journal,* June 1, 2001, p. C1.

- Roth IRA holders, who will be over age 59 1/2 during the year(s) of distribution, but whose accounts are insufficient to cover all college expenses,

- Taxpayers who will be under age 59 1/2 during the year(s) of distribution and will be paying expenses for college,

- Taxpayers who will be under age 59 1/2 during the year(s) of distribution and will be paying expenses for elementary and/or secondary education, and

- Taxpayers who choose to keep the funds in their Roth account for retirement purposes.

Other benefits of Coverdell Education Savings Accounts include:

1. The opportunity to roll benefits from one child to another, and

2. The opportunity to make contributions to cover services to be provided to special needs beneficiaries.

.01 Eligibility

The Coverdell Education Savings Account allows full contributions, $2,000 per year, for single individuals with modified adjusted gross income of up to $95,000 and for married couples filing jointly with adjusted gross income of up to $190,000. Beyond those amounts there are gradual phaseouts with no benefit available for single taxpayers with MAGI over $110,000 or married couples filing jointly over $220,000. Unusual provisions of the law may make it possible, however, to have the Coverdell account funded by a corporation or other entity without regard to income limitations. Further, friends, relatives, or even a child, who are within the allowable income thresholds could fund the account.[6]

.02 Qualified Education Expenses

Qualified education expenses eligible for tax-free distributions of funds generally includes tuition, fees, books, supplies, equipment, and room and board.[7] Such expenses, following amendment by the Economic Growth and Tax Relief Reconciliation Act of 2001, may now also include those incurred for elementary and secondary education, as well as for higher education.

TAX PLANNING: Even parents of elementary and secondary school students who do not attend private or parochial school may benefit from the allowances for technology. Expenses incurred, for example, for the purchase of computer equipment and/or the operation of high-speed Internet service are allowable. Importantly, these expenses do not have to be incurred exclusively for the benefit of the student. Instead, the expenses for technology simply must be "used by the beneficiary and the beneficiary's family during any of the years the beneficiary is in school."[8] Interestingly, the Code

---

[6] Code Sec. 530(c)(1) was amended to add the introductory phrase, "In the case of a contributor who is an individual," to clarify that other entities could make contributions without being subject to income limitations.

[7] Room and board will be treated as a qualified higher expense only if the student is enrolled on at least a half-time basis.

[8] Code Sec. 530(b)(4)(A)(iii).

does not address whether the child's use must be substantive. A literal reading of the rules would suggest that a parent could be the primary user of a computer and/or related Internet services, without disqualification or allocation of the amount expended.

.03 Limitations and Restrictions

As a starting point, the amount of distributions eligible for tax-exempt treatment must be reduced by scholarships[9] and certain other education allowances. This amount is then further reduced by expenses taken into account for the claiming of the Hope and/or Lifetime Learning Credit.[10] If this remaining amount is less than the amount expended for qualifying education expenses and no distributions have been made from a Section 529 Qualified Tuition Program, then no income is reported by the taxpayer.

> **Example 4:** *Tax Year 2004.* Tom and Tina Rose, a married couple filing a joint return, withdraw $8,000 from a Coverdell Education Account to pay their son's, Ted, college tuition and room and board. Tom and Tina's modified adjusted gross income is $160,000. The total cost of tuition and room and board, $15,000, has been reduced by a scholarship in the amount of $5,000. The remaining amount, $10,000 is covered by student loans. Tom's income is over the allowable threshold for claiming education credits (Hope or Lifetime Learning) or the deduction for college tuition. No amounts are withdrawn from a Section 529 Qualified Tuition Program or from tax-deferred U.S. savings bonds.

> The amount withdrawn by Tom and Tina, $8,000 is less than the maximum allowance of $10,000 [$15,000 - $5,000 scholarship] and, therefore, qualifies as a fully tax-exempt withdrawal. The computation of allowable amount is not affected by the student loan.

> **Example 5:** Same facts as in Example 4, except that Tom and Tina's income is $130,000. This income level would allow them to qualify for the full above- the-line tuition education expense deduction. Tom and Tina, without consideration of withdrawals from the Coverdell account could claim the full $3,000 tuition expense, since the qualifying expenses, $10,000 are more than the maximum allowance. Since, however, $8,000 has been withdrawn from the Coverdell account, only $2,000 can be claimed as a deduction.

> **Corrective action:** If Tom and Tina repay $1,000 plus related income earned by the first day of the sixth month of the following year to their Coverdell account, they will be able to claim the full $3,000 expense deduction.

> **PRACTICE POINTER:** The amount of distributions taken from a Coverdell account should be monitored to ensure that there is not an inadvertent

---

[9] Excluded from income under Code Sec. 117.

[10] Prior to 2002, Hope and Lifetime Learning credits could not be claimed in years where there were distributions from Educational IRAs.

loss of the tuition expense deduction. Taxpayers whose tax returns are on extensions could, in some cases, benefit from a review prior to June 1.

Example 6: Same facts as in Example 4, except that Tom and Tina's modified adjusted gross income is $80,000 and, therefore, low enough to claim a Hope Education credit. Their credit, $1,500, is based on a total of $2,000 in educational expenses [1st $1,000 x 100% and 50% x $1,000]. The maximum allowed as a tax-exempt withdrawal is $8,000 [$15,000 -$5,000 scholarship - $2,000 expenses taken into account for purposes of computing the Hope Scholarship].

If the amount withdrawn is more than the total qualified tuition expenses, $8,000, the taxpayer is potentially subject to tax and a ten percent penalty. The penalty would be assessed on a pro-rata portion of the excess distribution deemed to be from income. The fact that there are no remaining eligible education expenses for purposes of claiming the tuition education expense deduction is irrelevant, because no amount may be claimed for a tuition expense deduction in the same year that there is a claim for an education credit.

Corrective action: If Tom and Tina repay the excess Coverdell distribution and related income by the deadline date, normally June 1 of the following year, no tax or penalty will be assessed.

In cases where total distributions from a Coverdell account and a Section 529 qualified tuition plan exceed the amount of eligible expenses, an allocation must be made between the two.[11]

.04 Rollovers and Required Distributions

Examples 5 and 6, above, illustrate scenarios where corrective action could be taken to avoid imposition of tax and penalties for excess distributions from a Coverdell account. In some cases, however, it may be that funds are no longer required for the designated child's education expenses. Under such situations, taxpayers may wish to take advantage, where possible, of the opportunity to roll over funds to other family members. An important benefit of the rollover provisions is that they do not take into account the $2,000 annual limit.[12]

TAX PLANNING: The rollover provisions may be particularly helpful for increasing a fund for one child where another child will not require use of the fund (e.g., child awarded scholarship and/or stepchild supported by another parent).

Example 7: Alan and Elaine are planning to fund the college education of John, their four year old child. Jean, age 8, the daughter of Elaine and the stepdaughter of Alan, will have her college education funded by her father. Even though Jean will not require college funding, Alan and Elaine could annually fund a Coverdell account for her and then roll it over into John's account.

---

[11] Code Sec. 530(d)(2)(c).

[12] Code Sec. 530(d)(5).

TAX PLANNING: The rollover provisions can be utilized to extend the period for tax-free growth by rolling over unused portions of the IRA to the youngest child.

Example 8: Coverdell Savings Accounts are opened for two brothers, Bob and Barry, ages 7 and 2, respectively. Bob and Barry's parents could potentially achieve an additional five years of tax-exempt income by rolling over the funds in Bob's account to Barry's account.

If funds are not required by a beneficiary because tuition and/or room and board has been covered through the awarding of a scholarship or allowance,[13] then the 10 percent penalty will not be assessed. Taxes, however, will be assessed on the income portion attributable to the amount distributed. If funds remain in a beneficiary's account after she has reached age 30, they will generally be treated as being distributed 30 days after that date.[14] The income portion of such balances will be subject to tax and penalty.

TAX PLANNING: A taxpayer who does not use Coverdell funds for a qualifying purpose may find three potential problems: 1) penalty tax, 2) loss of 15 percent (or less) tax bracket for dividends and 3) loss of 15 percent (or less) tax bracket for capital gains. As a result, taxpayers who have some significant doubts as to whether funds in a Coverdell account will be used for qualifying purposes may choose not to invest in such accounts or do so only if 1) preponderance of the funds would be subject to ordinary income (e.g., bonds) and 2) the time before expected distribution is sufficiently long to provide significant tax-deferred compounding benefits. Also, if the parents expect to be in a lower tax bracket at the time of the required distribution, the Coverdell benefit may prove beneficial. Taxpayers, for example, may anticipate that at the time their child turns age 30, they will be retired and in a lower tax bracket.

TAX PLANNING: Parents may still benefit from the provisions allowing tax-free distributions for room and board, even in cases where there child is a commuter and/or attending college on a part-time basis. Up to $1,500/year may be claimed in qualifying room and board expenses for a child who resides at home with his parents or guardians and is attending college on at least a half-time basis.[15]

.05 Financial Aid Asset Categorization Issues

Coverdell Education Savings Accounts and Section 529 College Savings Plans owned by a student's parents receive equal treatment in the calculation of recommended financial aid. In both cases, the accounts are treated as assets of the parents. Also, nontaxable distributions from these accounts are not counted as parent or student income and, therefore, do not reduce financial aid eligibility. Prior to publication of U.S. Dept. of Education Letter: DCL ID: GEN-04-2,

---

[13] As defined under Code Sec. 25A(g)(2).

[14] Code Sec. 530(d)(8).

[15] Prop. Reg. § 1.529-1(c). This proposed regulation is actually written for Section 529 qualified

tuition programs. Code Sec. 530, Coverdell Savings Accounts in paragraph (b)(2) specifies that "qualified education expenses" means "qualified education expenses (as defined in Code Sec. 529(e)(3) . . . "

January 22, 2004, providing "clarification," Coverdell accounts were generally viewed as less favorable, for purposes of financial aid eligibility, than Section 529 College Savings Plans.[16]

¶803 Section 529 Qualified Tuition Programs May Be the Most Feasible Option for College Funding

Although Roth IRAs and Coverdell Savings accounts offer taxpayers the most flexibility for tax-exempt college funding, many taxpayers will find either that:

1. Their high incomes preclude them from participating in such vehicles, and/or

2. The Roth and Coverdell vehicles do not generate sufficient funds to cover the total cost of their beneficiary's education.

In such cases, Section 529 qualified tuition programs may be the most feasible option for college funding. Additionally, some taxpayers may actually prefer 529 plans over Roth or Coverdell accounts because they:

1. Prefer to have their college savings managed in accordance with a state plan, often at a lower cost than would be the case with other professional management,

2. Wish to avail themselves of a special gift-tax provision that allows for the tax-free front loading of a gift, or

3. Wish to avail themselves of state and local tax benefits available for contributions to in-state plans.

There are two types of qualified tuition programs:

1. Prepaid educational arrangements (PEAs), and

2. Educational savings accounts (ESAs).

PEAs generally allow parents or others to purchase future tuition credits or certificates, thereby allowing them to lock in tuition costs at current levels.

ESAs allow parents or others to choose among a variety of state-sponsored investment programs as a means of funding colleges.

A drawback of a Section 529 plan is that nonqualified distributions are subject to tax and penalty on the portion attributable to income. A number of opportunities are available, however, to allow contributors to avoid taking nonqualified distributions, through procedures for shifting funds amongst potential beneficiaries.

.01 Section 529 Plan Benefits

The primary tax benefit of Section 529 plans is that once funds are contributed, they are treated as tax-exempt, provided that the funds are used for a beneficiary's qualifying higher education expense. Such expenses include tuition,

---

[16] "Summary: Treatment of Coverdell Accounts and 529 Tuition Plans," *U.S. Dept. of Education Information for Financial Aid Professionals (IFAP) Library,* DCL ID: GEN-04-2, January 22, 2004.

fees, and the costs of books, supplies and equipment and room and board.[17] Noteworthy is the broad application of the term "qualifying" as it relates to the cost of education. The amount of eligible costs allowable in a single year could, for example, cover *five* years of actuarially determined expenses at the highest cost institution covered by a plan.[18] Alternatively, for lower spending beneficiaries, for example students who reside at home and commute to college, a $1,500 per student per year allowance for room and board is now available.

While, for many taxpayers, Section 529 plans will be the only viable means of tax-exempt college funding, for others, they will be an important supplement or, in some cases, an alternative to the limited opportunities afforded by Roth or Coverdell accounts. Roth accounts, for some taxpayers, even with the increased allowances, will be insufficient to cover college costs, either because such funds are actually earmarked for retirement and/or the actual costs of education are in excess of the funds accumulated in the Roth. Similarly, the benefits of Coverdell accounts may be limited by the $2,000/year cap on annual contributions.

.02 Front Loading of Gifts and Rollover Opportunities

An unusual gift-tax benefit applicable to Section 529 plans is a provision that allows individuals the opportunity to front-load gifts, absent application of gift taxes, of the first $55,000 in contributions for a designated beneficiary. A taxpayer may treat a $55,000 contribution as representing $11,000 gifts for the current and next succeeding four years. Married individuals with multiple beneficiaries can use the provisions to immediately remove significant sums from their future estates. Transfers between beneficiaries, without application of the gift-tax provisions, are allowable only for members of the same generation.

> **Example 9:** Andrew and Andrea Anderson, desire to contribute the maximum amount allowable to fund Section 529 plans for the following beneficiaries:
>
> Bob, son, age 15
>
> Carol, daughter , age 10
>
> Diane, niece, age 5
>
> Elaine, daughter-in-law, age 15[19]
>
> Andrew and Andrea, by employing gift-splitting, could together contribute $110,000 for each of the four beneficiaries, for a total of $440,000. Andrew and Andrea would not be able to make any additional gifts to those individuals that would qualify for the gift-tax exclusion during the five year period covered.
>
> **Example 10:** Ten years after their original contributions, Andrew and Andrea, transfer the funds from Bob, their older child's account to Carol, the

---

[17] Prop. Reg. §1.529-1(c).

[18] Prop. Reg. §1.529-2(i). The actual amount allowed will vary, depending on the rules of an individual state's plan.

[19] A complete list of eligible beneficiaries is contained in Prop. Reg. §1.529-1(c).

younger child. The transfer allows them to extend the period of tax-exempt growth without application of the gift tax.

Example 11: Eight years after the transfer to Carol, Andrew and Andrea seek to again transfer funds. This time they would like to shift the funds to Bob's child, Gale, a three-year old child. In this case, however, the amount of the transfer would be limited to $110,000, without incurring the generation-skipping transfer tax.[20]

.03 State Tax Considerations

A number of states provide tax benefits for residents who contribute to in-state programs. New York, for example, allows a deduction for contributions and an exclusion from earnings. The upfront benefit for contributing to an in-state program, such as New York's, can be substantial for high-income taxpayers.

Example 12: Sally contributes $10,000 to New York's in-state qualified tuition program, naming Sam, age 1, as her beneficiary. She is subject to the highest marginal tax rates for New York City residents, approximately 10 percent. Also, she is subject to the alternative minimum tax and gets no benefits for claiming state and local income taxes as an itemized deduction.

Assuming the $10,000 contribution earns an average rate of 8 percent per year, it would be worth $46,610 after twenty years. If she were to invest the equivalent out-of-state after-tax funds, $9,000, the account after twenty years would be worth $41,949. The net increase in value from the in-state program, therefore, is $4,661. If, for example, the rate of return were 12 percent, relatively typical of historical U.S. stock returns, the difference would be somewhat more dramatic. The in-state account would be worth $96,460, while the total for the out-of-state equivalent after-tax investment would be $86,814, a difference of $9,646.

TAX PLANNING: The benefit of in-state tax deductibility may be greatest, relative to out-of-state programs, where:

1. State and local tax rates are high,

2. Time horizon is short, and

3. Funds are invested conservatively.

Example 13: Wally and Wanda Wallace are subject to a federal tax rate of 27 percent and a state and local tax rate of 7.5 percent. The net current tax benefit of contributing to a deductible qualified tax plan, therefore, is 5.4 percent [7.5 − (.27 x .075)]. The Wallaces, depending upon actual college costs, anticipate that they will be using the funds within the next two to five years to pay for their daughter, Wendy's, college education. Since the funds are to be used in the near future, they would prefer that the bonds be invested in a conservative bond account.

---

[20] The five-year averaging rule of Prop. Reg. § 1.529-5(b)(2) is allowable for generation-skipping transfers under Prop. Reg. § 1.529(5)(b)(3)(ii).

The Wallaces are considering the following choices of investments:

1. $2,500 in a deductible state plan projected to yield 5 percent.

2. $2,365 in a nondeductible out-of-state plan projected to yield 6 percent. Investment, after-tax, is equivalent to amount invested in the in-state plan.

Value of Account	In-state	Out-of-state
End of Year 1:	$2,625	$2,507
End of Year 2:	2,756	$2,657
End of Year 3:	$2,894	$2,817
End of Year 4:	$3,039	$2,986
End of Year 5:	$3,191	$3,165

Even though the out-of-state account is projected to yield a tax-return that is twenty percent higher than the in-state return [6 percent per year instead of 5 percent], an unlikely scenario for an alternative bond investment of similar risk, a time period of as long as five years is still too short for the returns of the out-of-state return to compensate for the state tax deduction benefit of the in-state return.

PRACTICE POINTER: Evaluation of whether to use an in-state or out-of-state plan should also contain a careful analysis of operating expenses. At least a dozen states charge 2 percent or more for management of a Section 529 plan.[21] In some cases, such expenses may be expected to generate returns that would be less than what would be received, after-tax, from an account that is not part of a Section 529 plan. This may be particularly true when returns are compared for index-based stock and bond investments.

PRACTICE POINTER: Evaluation and comparison of the various state plans can be challenging because of the high number of alternatives and changes in structure and benefits. Some programs offer perks, for example, that can provide significant help, but only for relatively small groups of people. Virginia, as one case, lifts their normal cap on state deductibility of contributions of $2,000/contract per year for purchasers, age 70 and older.

A very helpful web site, wiredscholar.com/paying.content, a "product of Sallie Mae," prepared by Joseph F. Hurley, CPA, contains ratings of the programs, in terms of benefits for residents and for nonresidents. The program also contains links to each of the programs and allows for comparisons across relevant criteria (e.g., whether plan is fully open to nonresidents and whether in-state contributions are deductible for state tax purposes).

.04 Other Considerations

Uniform gifts to minors acts. Many, but not all states, allow transfers from custodial accounts established under the Uniform Gifts to Minors Act or Uniform Transfers to Minors Act into Section 529 programs. A limitation of utilizing this transfer, however, is that such funds cannot be transferred to another beneficiary.

---

[21] "Section 529 Crime Wave," by William Baldwin, *Forbes*, Dec. 8, 2003, Vol. 172 (12), p.24.

¶803.04

Further, if the funds transferred into the Section 529 account are ultimately not used for qualifying education expenses, a ten percent penalty will be applicable, as would be the case with any nonqualifying distribution of funds.

Programs offered by private institutions. Qualified tuition programs, effective in 2002, are no longer limited to state sponsored programs. Private institutions that meet certain requirements, including the holding of funds in a "qualified trust," can now offer prepaid tuition plans, although not savings programs of the type offered under state sponsorships. A potential drawback of investing in a prepaid tuition program offered by a private institution is that investors are precluded from also making contributions to qualifying Section 529 savings accounts. Another limitation is that distributions from plans offered by private institutions are not tax-exempt prior to 2004.

Financial incentives of advisers. Investments in Section 529 saving plans may be marketed by outside sales representatives. The use of these representatives may lead to some plans charging higher costs than funds that do not offer commissions or other compensation to outside sales people. Investors, therefore, should carefully consider the effects of costs in evaluating the potential long-term return of a plan.

Financial aid. Qualified Section 529 savings plans are treated as an asset of the parents, for financial aid purposes, while prepaid tuition benefits are not.[22] Further, prepaid tuition plans reduce a student's eligibility for financial aid on a dollar-for-dollar basis.[23]

.05 Interactions with Other Benefits

Deduction for higher education expenses. Distributions attributable to income from qualified tuition plans reduce the amount available for the higher education tax deduction. Distributions attributable to principal, however, do not reduce the amount of the eligible expenses.[24]

> **Example 14:** Jane Smith incurs $25,000 in qualifying educational expenses for her beneficiary during the year. The entire amount was paid with qualifying distributions. The amount of the distribution attributable to income was $15,000. Although all qualifying educational expenses were paid with distributions from the Section 529 plan, Jane still has $10,000 in expenses qualifying for the tuition expense deduction. Note that excludable distributions from U.S. savings bonds and/or Coverdell savings accounts could further reduce the amount eligible for the higher education expense deduction.

Hope Education and Lifetime Learning Credit. The full amount of distributions, including principal and earnings, attributable to education expenses taken

---

[22] Department of Education interpretation of the Higher Education Act of 1965. *See* 20 U.S.C. §1087kk-vv. Other information may be available at www.ed.gov and www.ifap.ed.gov.

[23] Reported and discussed in a) "Planning Strategies Under the Education Provisions of the New Tax Act," by Joseph F. Hurley, *Journal of Financial Planning*, Vol. 14-9, September 2001, pp. 116 – 128 and b)" My Painful Journey to Find the Best College-Savings Deal," by Terri Cullen, *Wall Street Journal Online*, July 18, 2001.

[24] Code Sec. 222(C)(2)(B).

into account for purposes of claiming the Hope Education or Lifetime Learning Credit reduce the amount available for the claiming of the exclusion for distributions from Qualified Tuition Programs.[25] If the amount distributed exceeds the allocable expenses, only the excess portion attributable to earnings will be includable in income.[26]

Coverdell Education Savings Accounts. If the total distributions from a qualified tuition plan and a Coverdell Education Savings account exceed the total qualified education expenses, taxpayers will be required to allocate expenses between the two vehicles. The IRS has not yet provided a formula for calculating the applicable allocations.

Savings bond interest. Excludable distributions from qualified plans reduce the amount of distributions from U.S. Savings Bonds, used for tuition expenses that would otherwise be exempt from taxation.[27] See ¶805 for discussion of exclusion of U.S. Savings Bond Interest.

Student loan interest. Excludable distributions from qualified plans reduce the amount of qualified education expenses that may be taken into account for calculating the amount of deductible student loan interest.

¶804 The EGTRRA Act of 2001 Provides Expanded Opportunities for Claiming Student Loan Interest Deductions

The deduction for student loan interest, an adjustment for adjusted gross income, is generally available where indebtedness is incurred solely on behalf of a taxpayer, spouse, or dependent (as described in Section 151), for qualified higher education expenses, subject to reductions described below, at an eligible educational institution. No deduction is allowable for qualified educational expenses where another income tax benefit has been claimed under the Code.[28] Further clarification of these requirements is presented below.

1. **Indebtedness incurred solely for qualifying higher education expenses.** A loan, for example, that was taken out for purposes of both a child's education and a parent's vacation would be disallowed in its entirety.

2. **Qualifying higher education expenses.** These expenses generally include tuition, fees, room and board, books, supplies, transportation and miscellaneous expenses.[29] This amount must be reduced by applicable scholarships.

3. **Eligible educational institution.** These institutions are generally certified by the U.S. Department of Education as being eligible to participate in student loan programs administered by the department.

The maximum amount allowable as a deduction is $2,500 and is not adjusted for inflation. In 2004, the phase-out ranges for individual taxpayers are between

---

[25] Code Sec. 529(c)(3).
[26] Code Sec. 529(c)(3)(B)(ii).
[27] Code Sec. 135(d)(2)(B).
[28] Prop. Reg. § 1.221-(g).
[29] Prop. Reg. § 1.221-1(f).

$50,000 and $65,000 for individual taxpayers and $100,000 - $130,000 for married couples filing joint returns.

TAX PLANNING: The general requirement that a taxpayer can only deduct interest expense in cases where he is obligated to make a payment is unchanged under the provisions allowing deductions of qualified student loan interest.[30] This could potentially result in the loss of deductibility in situations where a parent assumes loan payments made by the child.

The loss of tax deduction benefits may be mitigated, at least in part, in cases where parents or other individuals make gifts to the child who, in turn, directly pays the loan. This strategy may be beneficial even in situations where the child claims a standard deduction, since the student loan interest deduction is an adjustment for adjusted gross income. This strategy could also work in a reverse fashion, as might be the case where an adult child assumes the loans her parents incurred to pay for extended schooling (e.g., medical school).

¶805 Investments in I-Bonds Provide Potential Opportunities for Tax-Exempt College Funding with Flexibility

An exclusion of interest income is available for U.S. savings bonds redeemed by qualifying individuals for qualified higher education expenses. A benefit of holding these bonds, not available for Coverdell Education Savings accounts or Qualified Tuition Programs, is that no penalty is applied where the funds are ultimately not used for college. While the benefit for savings bonds is not restricted to I-bonds, their competitive interest rate and link to inflation may make them the optimal choice for some investors. The availability of the I-bond exclusion in the year 2004 is subject to a phaseout for married taxpayers filing joint returns with modified adjusted gross incomes (MAGI) between $89,750 and $119,750 and for other taxpayers with MAGI between $59,850 and $74,850. These amounts are adjusted for inflation.

In order for U.S. savings bond interest to be excluded from income the following requirements must be met:

- The U.S. savings bond must be issued after 1989,
- Bond must be issued to an individual at least age 24,
- Expenses incurred must be for the taxpayer, spouse or dependent (under Section 151), and
- Qualified education expenses must be reduced by scholarships, educational assistance allowances, and expenses taken into account for the Hope Credit, Lifetime Learning Credit, and the exclusion for distributions from qualified tuition plans.

PLANNING POINTER: I-bonds provide potentially significant benefits for taxpayers who would like flexibility to use funds either for college, retirement, or other purpose. If, for example, parents are reasonably confi-

---

[30] Prop. Reg. § 1.221-1(b)(1).

dent that they will be within the allowable income parameters at a future time when funds would likely be withdrawn for educational purposes, then there is little downside risk in holding this investment.

Example 15: Al and Alicia Larson, over a course of fifteen years save $80,000 in a Section 529 Qualified Tuition program and $20,000 in I-bond investments for the tuition of their only child, Arleen. The actual qualified costs of education are $85,000. Al and Alicia should use $80,000 from the qualified tuition program and $5,000 from the I-bonds. Al and Alicia can continue to hold the remaining $15,000 in I-bond investments until a future date. No penalty is applicable for the I-Bond not used for education.

.01 I-Bond's Benefit of Zero Commissions and Operating Costs Can Be Significant

A potentially significant benefit of purchasing I-bonds, as opposed to investing in a qualified tuition program is that no commission or operating costs are incurred.

Example 16: Lisa Liven invests $10,000 in a qualified tuition program and $10,000 in an I-bond. Each investment generates a 7 percent annual gross income but the qualified tuition program imposes an annual expense fee of 1 percent. After twenty years the value of the I-bond is $38,700, while the value of the holdings in the qualified tuition program is $32,071.

Note the impact of expenses on net returns for qualified tuition plans may take on increasing importance as qualified tuition plans increase costs in order to compensate for the use of commission sales people to market their product.

¶806 Financial Aid Considerations

The two major categories of financial aid are loans and grants. The benefits of loans for many taxpayers may only be significant if they are *subsidized*, whereby the debtor is not liable for interest incurred during the period of time the student is enrolled in college and for a short grace period, thereafter. Grants, alternatively, are the preferred form of financial aid because they reduce college costs on a dollar-for-dollar basis.

Families who would like to get a preliminary estimate of their expected financial contribution and how it might change depending on changes in assets and incomes may find it helpful to use a commercial and/or internet-based calculator or worksheet.[31]

PRACTICE POINTER: Clients should be advised that financial aid packages are often negotiable and may be adjusted, favorably, based on factors such as loss of a job or other extenuating circumstances.[32] Also, students who are deemed "desirable" by a college may, in some cases, be able to obtain financial aid packages that provide greater proportions of

---

[31] "How Much Aid Can You Expect?" provides a worksheet for estimating expected family financial aid contributions [smartmoney.com/college/finaid].

[32] "How to Negotiate for More Aid," at smartmoney.com/college/finaid provides a discussion of the negotiation process.

grants, rather than loans and work-study benefits.[33] Further, some colleges even encourage highly desirable students to show them their offers from other institutions so that they may have the opportunity to match or exceed them.[34]

Clients should be aware, however, that financial aid packages may be reduced in future years and, therefore, it may be helpful to ask financial aid officers for information as to what aid can be realistically expected beyond the first year.

.01 Perkins Loans

These loans are generally the most attractive because:

* Low fixed interest rate [5 percent],
* Subsidized during the period of academic enrollment and nine month grace period, and
* No origination fee is required.

The maximum annual amount that may be awarded to an undergraduate student each year is $4,000. Loans are also available for graduate and professional study. These loans may be the most difficult to obtain, however, because they are intended to be awarded only to students who exhibit exceptional financial need.

.02 Stafford Loans

These are variable rate loans for students with a cap on loan interest of 8.25 percent. Two forms of the loans are available: subsidized and unsubsidized. The subsidized loans are awarded based on financial need, while the unsubsidized loans can be awarded without regard to financial need. The benefit of the subsidized loan is that interest does not accrue during the time of college attendance or during the grace period before repayment. Unsubsidized loans require accrual of interest from the time that the loan is distributed. A potentially significant detriment of the Stafford Loan program is that loan origination fees of up to 4 percent may be imposed on the borrower.

.03 Federal Plus Loans

These are variable rate loans for parents with a cap on loan interest of 9 percent per year. The actual rate is adjusted annually. The rate for 7/1/03—6/30/04 is 4.22 percent. These loans, similarly to Stafford Loans, may also require the payment of an origination fee of up to 4 percent of the amount of the loan.

PRACTICE POINTER: Parents who can finance their children's education through home equity loans may find it may not be productive or, perhaps, may even be counterproductive to significantly shift assets and/or

---

[33] "Six Questions You Need to Ask About Financial Aid," Anonymous, *Money*, Volume 28, December 1999.

[34] "Spending It, Investing It—Matters of Degree: Echo Boomers are about to Hit College, and that may be Good News for their Cash-Strapped Parents," by David Franecki, *Wall Street Journal*, November 29, 1999.

adjust their investment practices for purposes of *potentially* enhancing their child's ability to qualify for subsidized student loans, payable by the student. Although the subsidized student loan allows students to avoid being charged for the accrual of interest while in college, the amount that can be borrowed during the first two years may be too small (e.g., Stafford loan is $2,625 for the first year and $3,500 for the second year) to compensate for a loss in investment return or deductibility of interest expense. After the second year, the amount for Stafford loans increases to $5,500 per year for undergraduates, but the amount of the deferral benefit may be reduced because of significant loan origination fees (e.g., 4 percent).

PRACTICE POINTER: Parents, prior to shifting assets, may wish to consider whether they have a realistic opportunity to obtain a subsidized loan. As an initial step, parents may find it helpful to investigate selected college's policies, including level of flexibility, for awarding student loans.

Note: In 1996, the 50th and 75th percentiles for income of all families of dependent students was $46,838 and $71,134, respectively.[35]

Parents who are considering utilizing PLUS loans for their children's education should be cognizant of the income-based eligibility restriction that would limit or even eliminate their ability to deduct student loan interest. Although such taxpayers may later have an opportunity to refinance these loans with home equity loans, they may regret that they incurred a significant loan origination fee to utilize the PLUS program. An important limitation of the PLUS program is that the loans, unlike many home equity loans, do not offer a fixed rate option.

.04 Merit Awards

Merit-based scholarships may provide the best opportunity for upper income taxpayers to receive financial aid. Scholarships, of course, are normally the most desirable form of financial aid because their benefits, when used for tuition, are tax-exempt and, unlike loans, they do not have to be repaid.

The awarding of merit aid is based on both an institution's financial resources and the competition for desirable students. Such students may not be limited to individuals with the highest grades and/or standardized test scores. They may, for example, include students who have demonstrated unusually strong leadership, musical talent or other attribute that could ultimately enhance a college's reputation. A detailed discussion of how colleges compete, through the awarding of merit scholarships, is beyond the scope of this book. A recommended article that may be helpful in understanding how colleges compete for such students, however, is "Welcome to the Bazaar," by Amy Dockser Marcus, *Money*, October 2001, pp. 112—120.

---

[35] "Trends in Student Borrowing: Subsidized and Unsubsidized Stafford Loans," *The Condition of Education 1999*, p. 215.

¶806.04

¶807 Long-Term Planning for Graduate Education

While many parents assume that their children, no matter how young, will eventually attend college, there is much more uncertainty as to whether they will attend graduate school. Nonetheless, with costs of graduate education (e.g., law school) potentially even greater than that for undergraduate education and generally with fewer opportunities for financial aid, it behooves parents to take such considerations into account when developing a long-term financial plan.

Example 17: John and Judy Devine, parents of Jason, age 2, would like to be financially prepared to potentially fund his graduate education. Despite Jason's young age, the Devines believe it is important to begin saving now because Jason could begin attending graduate school at a time shortly before the time they plan to retire. The amount of funds required for graduate education would, of course, depend upon the course of study (e.g., medical school), the specific school, and any potential financial aid.

John and Judy determine they would like to set aside funds to cover approximately three years of education, as might be required in the event that their son ultimately enrolls in law school. Assuming that the current cost for one year of law school is approximately $25,000 and inflation for education grew at a rate of approximately 5 percent/year the cost for the first year's education would be approximately $66,000. The three year total would be approximately $200,000.

Potential investment options include:

Qualified Section 529 tuition plan. The major potential benefit of these plans is that funds can be withdrawn on a tax-exempt basis for qualifying educational purposes. The major drawback, however, is that if the funds are not used for college, the amounts withdrawn could be subject to tax and penalty.

A nontax consideration for parents who are already using these plans for undergraduate education funding is that most have little or no track record. Parents may not want to cede direct investment control for both undergraduate and graduate education.

Exchange-traded shares. Investments in shares such as Standard & Poor's Depository Receipts (SPDRs) and/or American Stock Exchange Composites (QQQs) may be excellent vehicles for contingent investment planning. Such investments typically generate minimal current dividend income (approximately 1 percent or less) and normally have no or virtually no passthrough of capital gains.

Important long-term benefits include 1) long-term deferral of gain recognition allows increased compounding benefits, 2) capital gains, as well as qualified dividends, may qualify for 15 percent tax rates, and 3) opportunities to qualify for a 5 percent tax rate by shifting assets to a child who may be in a qualifying lower bracket.

Parents or others considering purchasing exchange-traded shares may wish to exercise additional caution when purchasing for long-term investing any type other than SPDRs or QQQs. Such shares could potentially have less long-term viability and, therefore, create additional financial and tax risks for the investor.

If a child does not attend graduate school, the parents may decide to continue to hold them and indefinitely extend the tax-deferral benefits of the investment. Additionally, if the shares are held until death, the investor could, depending upon the amount of his estate, avoid all taxes on the investment and potentially achieve a step-up in basis for his heirs.

A potential alternative to exchange-traded shares would be certain index funds. Index funds with low annual turnover, such as those based on the S&P 500, generally provide good opportunities to defer gains. A risk, however, not present with exchange-traded shares is that unusually large redemptions by other shareholders could lead to recognition of a fund's built-in gains.

Tax-managed funds. These funds also provide opportunities to defer a very high level of income until their redemption. At redemption, gains would normally be eligible for preferred five-year holding treatment. If funds are not used for college, they can be held indefinitely or even until death.

Potential concerns are:

1. Whether, over a long period of time, the tax management techniques will seriously constrain management's ability to generate good pre-tax returns, and

2. Whether, over a long period of time, management will be able to continue to effectively defer taxes, particularly if some event were to trigger a large-scale withdrawal of cash from the fund.

I-bonds. I-bonds may be excellent vehicles for long-term investing. Recognition of taxable income on I-bonds can be deferred for as long as thirty years. Also, if the funds are used for the education of a qualified dependent and parents meet the applicable income limitations, then all income is excluded.

TAX PLANNING: I-bonds may provide opportunities for individuals who will be retired while their children are attending college to take advantage of the exclusion for college expenses paid with U.S. savings bonds.

Example 18: Madelyn Meredith, age 42, is the mother of Michael, age 2. Madelyn currently earns $200,000/year and hopes to retire by age 62, at which point Michael could potentially be attending graduate school. She does not, however, anticipate drawing from her employer's pension plan or from Social Security until age 65, or later. She will fund the early stages of her retirement from dividends, distributions from her Roth IRA, and redemptions of high basis stock. She believes that it is entirely feasible that she can maintain her lifestyle in those early retirement years while maintaining a modified adjusted gross income level of under $57,600 (2002 allowable pre-phaseout income level, to be adjusted for inflation).

Madelyn assumes the current cost of graduate education is $25,000/year. Assuming a 5 percent level of inflation for education she would require approximately $66,000 to fund Michael's first year of graduate school. If she were to invest approximately $21,000 in both the current and following year she would have funds available to cover her son's expenses for the first two years of school when he would likely be ages 22 and 23 respectively. As a result of utilizing I-bonds for qualifying educational purposes, Madelyn would be able to exclude approximately $90,000 in interest income, over a two-year period.

Note that after age 23, Michael could qualify as a dependent only if his gross income was less than the exemption amount. Since the potential tax benefits are so large, Madelyn and Michael, as part of their plan would take steps to ensure that Michael's gross income does not exceed the exemption amount in any year that he is over age 23 and when she will be funding his education with I-bonds.

Caution when using I-bonds with gifts of stock or funds. Parents need to remember that the I-bond benefits apply only for educational expenses of a dependent. Therefore care should be taken not to have the child, himself, sell so large an amount of investments as to jeopardize parents' ability to claim the dependency exemption.

In the event that Michael does not go to graduate school, Madelyn still has the benefits of an investment that provides for as much as a thirty year deferral of income recognition and provides the benefit of matching inflation. This type of investment may be more attractive in states with high income taxes, because the U.S. savings bonds, in any event, are exempt from state income tax. This benefit may be even greater as more taxpayers become subject to the alternative minimum tax, in which case payments of state and local taxes would not be allowable as itemized deductions.[36]

---

[36] According to the Department of Treasury, Office of Tax Analysis Working Paper 87 (June 2000), 32 percent of taxpayers with incomes between $50,000 and $75,000 and four personal exemptions are expected to be subject to the alternative minimum tax in 2010.

Chapter 9

RETIREMENT FUNDING

¶901 Overview—Planning for Retirement Requires Preparing for the Unexpected

Four factors of uncertainty in planning for retirement can dramatically affect an individual's quality of life during the post-retirement years:

- Age at date of retirement,
- Age at date of death,
- Rate of inflation, and
- Market volatility.

The first factor, age at date of retirement, may appear to be largely under the control of the individual. A survey, however, conducted by the Employee Benefit Research Institute, found that 43 percent of retirees had to retire earlier than they had planned, largely because of poor health.[1] The second factor, date of death, is of course, normally not known with any precision. While, according to the IRS life expectancy charts, a 65 year-old individual is expected to live another 20 years, some will live longer and, of course, some will live shorter (although less of a retirement planning issue). Planning is further complicated where there are two spouses. Where there are two partners, the potential is greater for having at least one of them live well in excess of their IRS expected life span and, thereby, incur significantly greater retirement costs. The potential effects of inflation and market volatility are discussed in the following subsection. Consideration of all these factors is required to develop an appropriate context for developing a long-term tax-advantaged retirement plan.

.01 Inflation—The Most Significant Planning Concern for Many

The effects of inflation can potentially be so devastating that even individuals who, at first glance, may seem to be candidates for asset reductions for purposes of estate planning, may actually have a greater concern with increasing their assets in order to ensure that they may maintain their current lifestyles until the time of their deaths.

> **Example 1:** Abe, age 65, and Ally, age 60, retire in the current year. The couple's total assets are $2,000,000, most of which is in a fully taxable retirement account, the remainder of which is in bonds. They would like to draw about $120,000/year pre-tax, which is similar to what they were earning while they were both working.

---

[1] "Surprises Could Tarnish the Golden Years," by Eileen Ambrose, *The Sun*, October 24, 1999, p. 1D.

If Abe was to die at the exact IRS life expectancy rate of age 85 and inflation was to rise at a rate of 4 percent per year, the couple would require an annual income of approximately $263,000 in his final year of life to match, in real income, the $120,000 that was generated in the year of his retirement. If, however, he were to live to age 95, the current annual income required to meet the couple's lifestyle would be about $389,000.

If inflation were to rise at a rate of 6 percent per year, at Abe's age 85, the couple would require an annual income of approximately $385,000. At Abe's age 95, the couple would require an annual income of approximately $689,000.

Perspective-life expectancy. Life expectancy at the turn of the 20th century for an individual who was age 60, was only twelve years. Today, the fastest growing segment of the population is those aged 85 and older.[2] If such trends continue, reflecting advances in medical care, it may not necessarily be unrealistic to assume that an individual who is in his forties today, could well live into his nineties.

Perspective-inflation rate. The inflation rate from the end of 1939, just after the end of the Great Depression through the end of 1999, compounded at an annual rate of 4.3 percent. Inflation from 1960 to 1980 compounded at a rate of 6.2 percent. An additional factor to consider is that as people age, they may incur greater needs for health related services, whose costs may rise at a rate greater than the general rate of inflation.

Perspective-high inflation and stock performance. A factor potentially exacerbating the effects of inflation and further complicating planning is that stocks may be more likely to perform poorly during times of high inflation than at other times. In the decade of the 1970s, for example, while the compound rate of inflation was 7.4 percent, the compound rate of growth for S&P 500 was 5.9 percent. Thus, during the 1970s, the real rate of return for an investment in the S&P 500 was less than zero. Alternatively, where inflation has been low, stocks have generally performed well. In the 1950s, where inflation rose at a rate of 2.2 percent, the compound rate of return for large stocks was 19.4 percent.[3] In the 1990s, where the average inflation rate was 2.9 percent, the average return for the S&P 500 was 18.2 percent.

.02 Market Volatility—A Potentially Significant Disruptor for Long-Term Planning

While over the long-term stock investments have done well, with average returns over 11 percent for the period 1926-1999, short-term volatility may be large enough to seriously disrupt an investor's long-term plans, particularly, if she has the misfortune of beginning to draw upon retirement funds at a time of market decline.

---

[2] "Changing Retirement Age: Ups and Downs," by William J. Wiatrowski, *Monthly Labor Review*, April 2001, Vol 124-4, pp. 3-12.

[3] Return through February 1957 is based on the S&P Composite Index. Afterwards, the return is based on the restructured composite (S&P 500 Index).

Example 2: Carol Mead retired on September 30, 2000 with approximately $1,000,000 in retirement assets. She invested half of her assets in an S&P 500 based index fund, with rates of return subject to market fluctuations, and half in a fixed income investment, generating a 5 percent return per year. She plans to draw approximately $50,000 annually from her account. She believes her plan is a conservative one, because historically, stocks have generated annual returns of over 11 percent per year.

After one year, September 30, 2001, the value of the S&P 500 based index account has declined by approximately 27 percent. Her total investment portfolio, after taking into account a $50,000 withdrawal, $25,000 fixed income, and a $135,000 decline (27 percent) in her S&P based index fund is $840,000.

Even if the S&P 500, going forward, were to provide annual returns of 12.7 percent, its 10-year average return as of September 30, 2001, it would take her more than five years at that rate to get back to the starting point of $1,000,000, assuming she continues to draw only the $50,000/year. Also, even after the five years of favorable returns, there would be no real growth of principal after six years of retirement.

An important factor to take into account in developing a retirement plan is the client's attitude towards risk. Carol, after experiencing the large loss in the first year, may not want to risk having further reductions in principal. In that case, she would have to invest more conservatively and, therefore, reduce her style of living. Alternatives, such as investing more aggressively in an attempt to recapture market losses, may not be acceptable to many older taxpayers.

¶902 Stocks, Despite Risks, May Serve as Centerpiece for Long-Term Retirement Planning

Despite stock's inherent risks of vulnerability to inflation and market volatility they will serve, for many investors, as the most appropriate base for long-term retirement investing. The primary reason for investing more heavily in stocks, rather than in bonds, is simply that it may be very difficult for an investor to adequately fund her retirement through a portfolio consisting primarily of bonds.

During the period of 1926-1997 the compound annual return for the stock market was 10.6 percent, while for long-term government bonds the rate was 5.2 percent.[4] The difference in these returns, as illustrated in the following example, can have an extraordinary effect on an individual's retirement lifestyle.

Example 3: Three investors fund their retirement account at a rate of $10,000/year. The first investor's retirement account is funded 100 percent with bonds that compound at a rate of 5 percent per year. The second investor's retirement account is funded fully with stocks that compound at a

---

[4] *Stocks for the Long Run* by Jeremy J. Siegel, McGraw-Hill, New York, 1998.

rate of 10 percent/year. The third investor's retirement account is funded each year with 60 percent stocks and 40 percent bonds.

Time Frame	Investor #1 100% Bonds	Investor #2 100% Stocks	Investor #3 60% Stocks & 40% Bonds
24 Years	$445,000	$885,000	$708,990
36 Years	$958,360	$2,991,000	$2,178,106

Where retirement investments are held primarily outside of the retirement account, stocks have advantages over bonds of providing for long-term tax deferral and income recognition at favorable capital gains rates.

Example 4: Two investments of $10,000 each earn ten percent/year. Investment #1 is taxable currently at a combined state and local income tax rate of 20 percent. Investment #2 is also taxable at a combined income tax rate of 20 percent, but taxable income is not recognized until redemption.

Time Frame	Investor #1 20% Tax Rate Recognized Anually	Investor #2 20% Tax Rate Recognized at Redemption
10 Years	$21,600	$22,800
20 Years	$46,600	$55,800
30 Years	$100,600	$141,600
40 Years	$217,200	$364,100

Forms of stock investment that can potentially provide excellent opportunities for long-term tax deferral include:

1. Exchange-traded shares,
2. S&P 500 based index funds, and
3. Individual shares of growth stocks.

PRACTICE POINTER: Examples, such as the one above, may help clients better understand the value of deferring the recognition of income over extended periods of time. Many clients may be surprised to find that over extended periods of time, the benefits of tax deferral will often exceed the benefits derived from a reduction in tax rates.

¶903 Fixed-Return Investments Can Help Mitigate Risk, but May Reduce Returns

Empirical evidence suggests that the vast majority of long-term retirement assets should be stocks. According to Jeremy Siegel, professor of finance at the Wharton School of Business and author of *Stocks for the Long Run*, "for long term savings . . . eighty to ninety percent [in stocks] is not an unreasonable number."[5]

Alternatively, Roger Ibbotson, professor of finance at Yale University and chairman of Ibbotson Associates, a leading firm in the field of asset allocation, states "It's very easy to say you come out ahead if you sit it out for 20 years, but after five years of poor returns its very difficult to do that for many people."[6]

---

[5] "Bonds Let You Sleep at Night but at a Price,"   [6] *Ibid.*
by Ruth Simon, *Wall Street Journal*, September 8,
1998, p. C1.

The issue, discussed in more detail in an article by Ruth Simon in the *Wall Street Journal*,[7] is how much potential return is an investor willing to forego in order to maintain an acceptable level of comfort. An example, presented in that article, compared returns of a 100 percent stocks portfolio and a 60 percent stocks/40 percent bonds portfolio. Over a twenty year period, the 60/40 allocation would provide only 62 percent of the return of a 100 percent stock portfolio.[8] The comfort provided by that portfolio, however, may be significant and is well illustrated by the fact that during the period 1945 – 1997, the 60/40 portfolio incurred no losses in a single year greater than 15 percent and in only one year incurred a loss of greater than ten percent. In contrast, the 100 percent stock portfolio generated losses of greater than ten percent in six years, including one greater than 15 percent and one greater than 10 percent.

PRACTICE POINTER: Before developing any plan as to how to allocate assets for maximum after-tax returns, it is *highly* important to develop an apportionment program that the client feels that he can be reasonably comfortable with throughout the long-term retirement plan. If a plan is developed with unrealistic assumptions, the related tax-planning strategies can be easily undermined. Two common attributes of the nervous investor that can undermine an otherwise well developed long-term tax planning strategy include:

1. Sale of Stocks During a Market Downturn

    - Incur permanently nondeductible losses on sales in retirement accounts,

    - Incur currently nondeductible losses on sales in taxable accounts, where net losses are in excess of the annual allowance,

    - Recognize capital gains at ordinary income rates or at maximum 20 percent rate, rather than at reduced rates available for assets held more than five years, and

    - Lose tax deferral and related compounding benefits for assets sold prior to retirement.

2. Purchase of Stocks After the Market Has Recovered

    - Incur opportunity costs—lost opportunity to benefit from stock's appreciation at long-term capital gain rates, and

    - Subject higher portion of income to ordinary tax rates, assuming that ordinary income type investments, such as bonds, are held during the period of market recovery.

---

[7] *Ibid.*

[8] Baseline is average returns for the period 1945–1997.

¶904 Unconventional Approach to Asset Apportionment for Retirement Planning May Yield Significant Benefits

Once determinations have been made regarding a client's attitudes towards risk and his long-term goals, decisions must be made regarding the types of assets to be held and how to apportion them between taxable and tax-deferred or tax-exempt accounts. This section examines the issues involved in the apportionment of investment assets.

A study by Samuel F. Beardsley, a tax specialist at T. Rowe Price, found that an unconventional approach to the apportionment of retirement assets, placing bonds in taxable accounts and stocks in tax-deferred or tax-exempt accounts may often generate higher net after-tax income than the more conventional investment approach (i.e., place bonds in the tax-deferred or tax-exempt account).[9]

The conventional approach to retirement investing has been to place bond funds in tax-deferred accounts because these assets, where unsheltered, typically generate all or almost all of their income at ordinary tax rates. The flip side of the conventional approach has been to place stock funds in accounts that are not tax-exempt or tax-deferred because such investments can potentially be taxed at preferred long-term capital gains rates.

Amongst the findings of the Beardsley study is that over a twenty year period, January 1, 1981–December 31, 2000, for both growth and growth and income funds, the unconventional approach generated superior *after-tax* returns, as shown below.

Initial Investment: $10,000

Stock Fund Category	Unconventional Bond Funds–Taxable Stock Fds.–Tax Defd	Conventional Bond Funds–Tax Defd Stock Funds–Taxable
Growth	$149,100	$142,600
Growth & Income	$136,100	$130,100

The pre-tax results are based on the actual returns for the two categories as compiled by Morningstar Inc. The after-tax returns are based on a 28 percent ordinary income tax rate and a 20 percent long-term capital gains rate. The advantage for the unconventional approach was also found to be applicable where the taxpayer's ordinary income tax rate was 31 percent.

The reason presented for the results is essentially that the appreciation of stock funds was so great, relative to the bond funds, that a preferred 20 percent long-term capital gains rate was not sufficient to offset the magnitude of the income. The author also found that the effect of the unconventional approach would have been even greater had it been employed with a Roth IRA.[10]

---

[9] "Deciding Which Funds to Hold in Taxable vs. Tax-Deferred Accounts," by Samuel F. Beardsley, *www.troweprice.com/taxstrategy/decide.html.*

[10] Roth IRAs were not in existence as of the beginning of the time period studied.

There were some scenarios, however, where the conventional approach was found to be superior to the unconventional approach. In general, the shorter the time horizon and the higher the ordinary income tax bracket, the more likely it was that the conventional approach would provide a more advantageous return. Other situations where the conventional approach was more likely to provide the greater advantage were:

1. The retirement account was to be liquidated within 15 years, and

2. The stock fund investment was comprised of index funds.

In general, the more tax-efficient is the stock fund, the more beneficial it becomes to follow the conventional approach and place it, rather than a bond fund, in a taxable account.

PRACTICE POINTER: The Beardsley study highlights the importance of collecting, for retirement planning purposes, more detailed data regarding the tax-efficiency of fund investments (e.g., low turnover stock-index fund), the taxpayer's expected holding period until withdrawal, and assumptions regarding expected future pre-tax returns. If the client prefers more certainty and/or is more comfortable with the conventional approach (e.g., holding stocks in taxable accounts), then it may be more beneficial to hold stocks in highly tax-efficient vehicles, such as exchange-traded funds (e.g., SPDRs), where there is an expectation of no or virtually no passthrough of current capital gains.

PRACTICE POINTER: The benefits of the alternative approach presented in the Beardsley study may be lessened under current tax law where, in most cases, there will be at least a ten percent spread between ordinary income and capital gains rates (e.g., ordinary marginal rate of 25 percent and capital gains/dividends rate of 15 percent). If, however, the reduced tax rates applicable to capital gains and dividends rates actually expires, as scheduled for tax years beginning after December 31, 2008, the spread between ordinary income and capital gains/dividends rates could shrink to a size that would potentially make the alternative strategy more beneficial than it was under the prior system, where capital gains were taxed at a 20 percent rate.

¶905 Long-Term Care Insurance Can Reduce Risk and Provide Tax Benefits

A determination as to how to allocate assets for retirement should include consideration of long-term contingencies, such as the potential need for long-term care. If, for example, an investor does not have long-term care insurance he may seek to invest more conservatively in order to increase the probability that he will have funds to meet such needs. Insurance premiums for long-term care coverage, subject to limitations, are deductible as medical deductions. Self-employed individuals, however, subject to a phase-in, may receive an extra benefit by deducting premiums as an adjustment to income, even where they would not receive any benefit from its being claimed as an itemized deduction.

Example 5: Sarah Parker, age 65 and self-employed, pays an annual premium of $2,500 for long-term care insurance. The maximum amount of the premium subject to deductibility for an individual age 61–70 is $2,510 [2003 amount, adjusted for inflation]. As a self-employed individual she would be allowed to deduct 100 percent of the insurance premium, subject to her age-group maximum. Prior to 2003, self-employed individuals were not entitled to the full amount of medical insurance (e.g., 70 percent limitation in 2002).

Perspective: As life spans continue to grow, so may the need for long-term care. For example, while in 2000 approximately 4 million Americans were suffering from Alzheimer's disease, this amount is expected to triple to 12 million by the year 2050.[11] Additionally, for individuals who live past age 85, the probability of developing some form of dementia is 35 percent.[12] While all such individuals will not require full-time skilled nursing care, many will be in need of some type of assisted care.

Another consideration complicating retirement planning is that long-term care may be required prior to age 65. According to Phyllis Shelton, president of LTC Consultants, forty percent of the people who require long-term care are ages 18–64. She cited, as examples, the cases of *Christopher Reeves* and *Michael J. Fox*, who require long-term care as a result of an accident and a disease, respectively.[13]

PRACTICE POINTER: In cases where a client's health begins to deteriorate, planning considerations may include the need to simplify the components of an investment portfolio. If, for example, financial responsibilities are to be transferred to a spouse who has had no or minimal experience with such matters, it may make sense to do some consolidation of assets, such as reducing the number of open mutual funds. This strategy can be executed, from a tax perspective, potentially more effectively where there is a longer time frame, because there will be more latitude for choosing specific assets for liquidation.

¶906 Roth vs. 401(k) and/or Traditional IRA—Optimal Funding Choice Dependent Largely on Tax Brackets and Need for Flexibility

In general, most taxpayers will receive a greater tax benefit from funding a 401(k) and/or traditional IRA than from funding a Roth IRA, in cases where a taxpayer's marginal tax bracket will decline at the time of the distribution phase. A taxpayer, for example, who is currently subject to a 25 percent tax rate, but anticipates that he will be in a 15 percent tax bracket at time of retirement, would receive a tax benefit that would not be received by someone who contributes to a

---

[11] Projection according to the Alzheimer's Association, in "How to Keep Your Memory Intact," by Catherine Arnst, *Business Week*, October 15, 2001, pp. 128E4.

[12] "Piecing Together Alzheimer's," by Peter H. St. George-Hyslop, *Scientific American*, December 2000, Vol. 283-6, pp. 76–83.

[13] "Helping Hands: Long-Term Care Insurance has Never been an Easy Pill to Swallow: A Leading Expert Explains Why that's Changing," by Glenn Ruffenach, *Wall Street Journal*, October 22, 2001, p. R12.

Roth IRA. The holder of the Roth investment, however, has greater flexibility than the holder of a 401(k) or traditional IRA, because he would not be subject to minimum distribution rules.

.01 Overloading Roth Accounts, to Exclusion of Other Plans, May Potentially Cause Loss of Tax Benefits

Taxpayers, evaluating whether to contribute to Roth accounts or 401(k)/ traditional IRAs should be careful to plan to ensure that they receive the benefit of the reduced fifteen percent tax bracket.

Example 6: In 2004, Glen and Marie Jameson, each age 54, begin contributing $3,500/year into their Roth IRAs. They continue contributing $7,000/year, total, for ten years. Their marginal tax rate is 25 percent and their investments earn 12 percent/year. They plan on using these funds to fund their first three years of retirement, after which they will begin collecting fully taxable benefits from a pension plan for which they did not make contributions.

After ten years the total value of the Roth accounts are approximately $123,000. In the three years that they will draw on their account, other taxable income is anticipated to be only a nominal amount. As a result of this strategy, the taxpayers have lost the opportunity to benefit from the 15 percent and perhaps, even 10 percent tax bracket.

Alternatively, the couple, instead of contributing to the Roth accounts, could have contributed $9,300, assuming a marginal tax-rate of 25 percent, to their employers' 401(k) plans. Assuming that this income would be subject to tax at a 15 percent rate, the net after-tax amount would increase to approximately $139,000, or about $16 000 more than was generated bv the Roth account.

.02 Roth's Flexibility May Allow Taxpayers to Take Advantage of Other Tax Saving Benefits

The flexibility afforded by Roth IRAs may allow taxpayers to time distributions in order to avail themselves of other tax benefits.

Example 7: Joan Harrison, age 46, invests $3,000/year for 20 years in a Roth IRA. The account earns an average return of 10 percent /year. At age 66 she retires, at which point the value in the account is approximately $172,000. Joan also has substantial amounts invested in a corporate retirement plan.

Joan estimates, based on Social Security cost-of-living adjustments of approximately 3-4 percent/ year, that she will be eligible to draw about $30,000/year from Social Security. She estimates, based on similar inflation estimates that she will require approximately $115,000/year in after-tax income to meet her desired retirement goals.

Joan could potentially fund the first two years of retirement by drawing $85,000 from her Roth account and $30,000 from Social Security without having any of the $30,000/year in Social Security benefits be subject to tax. Without the Roth she could potentially be subject to a maximum 85 percent inclusion, $25,500/year of taxable social security benefits. See also ¶911 and ¶912 for more information on planning with Social Security benefits.

Other areas where she could potentially benefit from a reduced AGI include education credits, deductibility of medical expenses, and the child tax credit.

.03 Roth IRAs for Children—Flexible Options for Shifting, Deferring, and Excluding Income

Parents who are either ineligible or who have fully funded their own Roth IRAs, may find that funding a child's Roth IRA can provide significant potential tax benefits.

1. Income that is withdrawn by the child for qualified education purposes may be withdrawn penalty-free,[14] often at substantially reduced rates of tax.

Example 8: Mike Miller, a taxpayer in the 35 percent marginal tax bracket, provides his daughter Marcy, age 16, with $3,000 to fund her own Roth IRA.[15] The account generates income of 10 percent/year. He continues the funding pattern for eight years. At Marcy's age 24, the account is worth $34,308 and is liquidated to pay for one year of graduate school. While the income component drawn from the Roth IRA is subject to income tax, much of it will be at the 10 percent and 15 marginal rates. Mike, therefore, benefits by 1) deferral of income recognition; and 2) income recognition at lower marginal tax rates.

Assuming Mike is willing to cede control of the money, there is no financial detriment to the income shift. The 10 percent penalty, otherwise applicable for distributions made prior to the year in which the taxpayer is age 59 1/2, does not apply because the distribution is used for qualified education purposes. Also, since the funds are not being used for her support during the eight years in which the account is growing, it should not affect Mike's ability to qualify to claim her as a dependent.

TAX PLANNING: Eligible parents who have not fully funded their own Roth IRA accounts may consider doing so for contingent funding of their children's graduate education. Interestingly, distributions can be made, penalty-free, even in cases where the child is no longer eligible to be claimed as a dependent (e.g., child is age 24 or over). Other potential beneficiaries for penalty-free withdrawals include the taxpayer, his spouse, and grandchildren. Other individuals, who do not meet the limited relationship test, even if categorized as a dependent, do not qualify for this benefit.[16]

---

[14] Reg. §1.408A-6, Q & A 5(a) and Code Sec. 72(t)(2)(E).

[15] The example assumes that she has sufficient earned income to qualify for contributions to the IRA.

[16] Code Sec. 72(t)(7)(A) provides that eligible individuals include the taxpayer, spouse and any child (as defined in Code Sec. 151(c)(3)) or grandchild of the taxpayer or taxpayer's spouse who incur qualified higher education expenses (as defined in Code

2. Funds that are contributed to Roth IRAs during an individual's younger ages can provide extraordinary opportunities, through long-term tax-exempt compounding, to significantly fund an individual's retirement.

Example 9: The facts are the same as in the preceding example, except Marcy does not withdraw the funds from the account, and the investment continues to grow at a rate of 10 percent/year. The value of the account at age 60 would be approximately $1,060,000. This computation assumes that no contributions were made after Marcy was age 24.

PRACTICE POINTER: The benefit of the early funding can be demonstrated to a client by providing a comparison of how much money would accumulate in the account if, instead, the child were to begin funding the account herself at age 24, with $3,000 per year. The illustration would show that after 36 years of funding, her total account balance, approximately $897,000, would still be significantly less than the $1,060,000 that she accumulated from her father's eight years of contributions.

¶907 Nondeductible IRAs Provide Tax-Deferral Benefits and Potential Rollover to Roth

Taxpayers whose income is too high to qualify for the Roth IRA may benefit from the tax-deferral feature of nondeductible IRAs. Additionally, taxpayers whose income is currently too high to qualify for Roth IRAs, but whose income could later be reduced below the AGI threshold for one year, as in the first year of retirement, could potentially obtain its benefits through the Roth rollover provisions.

Although a nondeductible IRA is not as attractive as a Roth, where earnings are tax-exempt, the tax-deferral feature can be significant in cases where the investment would otherwise be taxed at ordinary income rates. A nondeductible IRA effectively has the same tax-deferral benefit of a variable annuity without the detriment of annuity operating expenses. While prior to enactment of the EGTRRA of 2001, many taxpayers may have considered the contributions limit too small to be worthwhile, the expanded contribution limits, especially for those age 50 or over, may provide viable opportunities to defer earnings recognition on significant levels of contributions. Beginning in 2008, for example, a couple with both spouses age 50 or over, may contribute a total of $12,000/year.

TAX PLANNING: Taxpayers considering using nondeductible IRAs should weigh the tax deferral benefit against the loss of any potential long-term capital gains treatment (e.g., 15 percent maximum tax rate). A taxpayer, for example, who would be investing in exchange-traded shares, where there is very little current recognition of taxable income, may find that a nondeductible IRA is not advantageous since the income, when recognized on distribution, would be at ordinary rather than at preferred long-term capital gains rates.

(Footnote Continued)

Sec. 529(e)(3)) at an eligible education institution (as defined in Code Sec. 529(e)(5))1.

In cases where the investor is planning on holding corporate bonds to maturity, the tax deferral feature of the nondeductible IRA may be very beneficial. In situations where there is a potential mix of ordinary income and capital gains (e.g., real estate investment trusts and utility stocks), the investor should probably run the numbers to see which avenue is the most promising.

.01 Nondeductible IRA May Serve as a Gateway for Roth

Taxpayers whose incomes are too high to qualify for Roth IRAs may, nonetheless, be able to use nondeductible IRAs as a gateway to Roth accounts.

Example 10: Toni, age 55, currently earns $200,000/year and, therefore, is ineligible to contribute to a Roth IRA. She contributes $3,500/year into a nondeductible IRA until age 65, at which point she retires. The investment earns 10 percent/year resulting in a valuation of approximately $56,000 at retirement. Although Toni, in most years including those after retirement, will have income over $100,000 she finds it is relatively easy to reduce her AGI to under $100,000 for one year to allow for a Roth IRA conversion. Toni accomplishes the one year income reduction largely by:

1. Deferring the taking of any distributions from retirement accounts or Social Security,

2. Funding her current lifestyle while liquidating investments having minimal or little built-in gains, and

3. Replacing liquidated investments, at least temporarily, with investments generating no current taxable income (e.g., municipal bonds or minimal taxable income (e.g., exchange-traded shares).

Toni rolls over the $56,000 in her nondeductible IRA into a Roth IRA. Importantly, while she is required to pay taxes on the conversion, she is still able to transfer the full amount of the principal into the Roth IRA. Further, any taxes paid on the rollover will have the effect of reducing her gross estate.

If the Roth IRA investment continues to earn 10 percent/year and is held for another twenty years, until Toni is age 85, the investment would be worth approximately $377,000. Toni, therefore, would have been able to exclude $321,000 in income from taxes. This benefit is in addition to the $21,000 in pre-retirement contribution for which she received at least some tax deferral benefit.

PRACTICE POINTER: Clients presented with tax deferral benefits only, may not be able to appreciate the long-term value of initiating contributions into a nondeductible IRA. A $21,000 tax-deferral, for ten years worth of investing, as in the above example, may seem like a minor matter to an individual of significant income and/or net worth. If, however, the client can see that such investments can set the framework for significant tax-exclusion benefits, then she may be more likely to avail herself of such opportunities.

¶907.01

¶908 One Person 401(k) Provides Opportunities for Increased Retirement Contributions

The Economic Growth and Tax Relief Reconciliation Act of 2001 eliminated the rule requiring that elective employee deferrals be included in computing the maximum amount that employers and employees can contribute to a 401(k) plan. This change in the law creates opportunities for sole proprietors to increase the total amount of funds they can annually contribute to their retirement plans. Under prior law the maximum combined contribution for employee and employer was 15 percent of $170,000. Under EGTRRA, for tax years beginning after December 31, 2001, an individual, as an employer, can contribute a maximum of 25 percent of $200,000, after taking into account the contributions, plus as an employee, he can contribute an additional $11,000/year. If the taxpayer is over age 50, he will also be eligible to increase the amount of the deferral through the "catch-up" provisions.

¶909 I-Bonds May Provide Excellent Opportunities for Long-Term Deferral of Income

I-bonds may provide investors with excellent opportunities to achieve both tax deferral and state tax benefits for the more conservative portion of their portfolios. These bonds, which have a fixed component that lasts for as long as the bond is held, and a variable component that is adjusted semi-annually based on the Consumer Price Index for all Urban Consumers, can provide tax-deferred growth for as long as thirty years. Alternatively, if the investor desires, the bond can be cashed at any time after five years without penalty. Bonds held for less than five years are subject to a penalty of three months loss of earnings.

I-bonds, as are all U.S. Savings Bonds, are exempt from state and local taxation.

> **Example 11:** Comparison of after-tax returns of certificates of deposits and I-bonds for an investor who is in a 25 percent federal bracket and a net 5 percent state bracket for a $50,000 investment. The annual pre-tax rate of return is assumed to be 5 percent.

After-tax Returns

Time Frame	Certificate of Deposit	I–Bond
10 Years	$70,500	$73,600
20 Years	$99,500	$112,000
30 Years	$140,300	$174,600

Even better returns for the I-bonds may be achieved in cases where the taxpayer is at a lower marginal tax bracket, as might well be the case after an individual retires from work. The benefits of the I-bond are less valuable in states where there is no or minimal state income tax.

> **PRACTICE POINTER:** The difference in protection between FDIC insurance for bank deposits under $100,000 and U.S. government backing for I-bonds may be minimal. Clients should keep in mind, however, that the

value of CDs held for an extended period of time may rise above the $100,000 threshold, which is not adjusted for inflation, and become subject to a loss of deposit protection. Clients, who prefer the fixed returns of a CD, may need to be reminded of the limits of FDIC protection and alternative means of obtaining that protection: 1) hold separately titled accounts at the same institution and/or 2) hold accounts at different institutions.

Investors who would like to investigate the financial condition of a potential bank, thrift or credit union may be able to access that information through an online service. One potential source of information, Bankrate.com's Safe & Sound Bank, Thrift and Credit Union Ratings, is available at *www.bankrate.com/brm/ safesound/ss_home.asp*.

.01 I-Bonds May Not Be Optimal Choice for Tax-Deferred Accounts

I-bond income, without the shelter of a retirement account can be deferred for up to thirty years. Alternatively, if an I-bond is held in a tax-deferred retirement account and the taxpayer is subject to minimum distributions, it will increase the amount of required current taxable distributions, without any current generation of cash.

¶910 Treasury Inflation Protection Securities (TIPS) May Be Preferable to I-Bonds for Tax-Exempt or Tax-Deferred Retirement Accounts

TIPS, historically, have been generating higher total income returns than I-bonds and, therefore, may be more advantageous to hold in tax-exempt retirement accounts. TIPS, from a practical perspective, may also be more advantageous to hold in retirement accounts that are subject to required minimum distributions. TIPS can provide a steady source of inflation-adjusted cash payments that can be used for distributions, while also providing for inflation-based adjustments to principal. I-bonds, alternatively, while providing for tax-deferral, do not generate any cash until redemption.

The fixed interest rate component for a new TIPS is set at a Treasury Department auction. The principal portion is adjusted semi-annually based on the non-seasonally adjusted U.S. City Average All Items Consumer Price Index for all Urban Consumers (CPI-U), published monthly by the Bureau of Labor Statistics.

> **Example 12:** Ray purchases $100,000 of TIPS at auction to be held in his traditional individual retirement account. Six months later the principal amount of the bond is adjusted to take into account two percent inflation that has occurred during the six months since he purchased the bond. Ray's security will earn interest at a fixed rate of three percent for the next six months based on a principal amount of $102,000. The amount of the required distribution in the IRA will be based on the total undistributed value in the account.

¶909.01

If Ray had, instead, invested in I-bonds for his IRA, he likely would have generated lower interest income and would not have generated any cash that could be used for the distribution.

PRACTICE POINTER: As of October 31, 2001, there are no planned issues of 30-year TIPS or nominal Treasury bonds. Although the Treasury Department has not indicated that they will also be discontinuing the 10-year TIPS, some institutional investors have expressed concern that these securities will also be discontinued because:

1. An advisory board to the Treasury Department believes their costs are too high for the government to justify offering additional issues, and

2. Discontinuance would provide better liquidity for the smaller group of remaining nominal Treasury securities.[17]

Taxpayers who are interested in this type of investment, therefore, may wish to consider the following courses of action

1. Purchase additional TIPS while still available, and

2. Purchase additional I-bonds; if TIPS are discontinued, leaving I-bonds as the only government backed inflation-adjusted security, it may be more likely that purchase costs for those bonds will increase and yields will decrease.

.01 Inflation-Adjusted Bond Funds May Undermine Inflation Protection

Some clients may express interest in acquiring inflation-adjusted securities through a fund, rather than by individual purchase. These funds, however, typically are not desirable investments for individuals whose primary concern is inflation protection. Since the net asset value of these funds can actually decline as a result of various economic conditions, these funds can actually be more speculative than protective in nature. Clients considering investing in such funds should be made aware of the potential risk that they may not achieve desired inflation protection.

¶911 Lump-Sum Election for Company Stock Distribution May Provide Capital Gains Treatment for "Net Unrealized Appreciation" and Future Appreciation

The Jobs and Growth Tax Relief Act of 2003 (JGTRRA) makes the election to take a lump sum distribution of company stock held in a 401(k) or an employee stock ownership plan (ESOP) an optimal choice for more taxpayers. There are at least four important benefits associated with this choice:

1. Any increase beyond the employee's basis will be subject to tax at capital gains rates, in contrast to ordinary income rates that are normally

---

[17] "TIPS' Cost Casts Cloud on Survival Prospects," by Vineeta Anand, *Pensions & Investment*, July 23, 2001.

applicable to retirement distributions.[18] The change in tax rates under JGTRRA means that taxpayers may be subject to tax rates of 15 percent or less for any appreciation beyond the employee's basis, regardless of holding period. Long-term employees and/or employees whose company stock has experienced significant appreciation stand to benefit the most from this provision.

2. Upon lump-sum distribution there is no requirement to make any further taxable distributions, as would be the case for investments held in a qualified retirement plan.

3. The shareholder, upon distribution, may sell some or all of the company stock and still qualify for long-term capital treatment on the net unrealized appreciation. Sale of company stock followed by reinvestment into other holdings can allow for diversification of the individual's portfolio, a potentially critical concern for long-term employees whose retirement assets are comprised predominantly of stock issued by their employer.

PRACTICE POINTER: While the benefits of compounding are reduced by selling company stock at time of distribution, rather than in the future, clients should be reminded that such benefits may be outweighed by risks associated with lack of diversification. This point should be particularly emphasized for clients whose retirement portfolio is or would be comprised primarily of employer issued stock.

4. Dividends from company stock or from qualifying stock purchased after the disposal of company stock qualify for tax rates of 15 percent or less. Alternatively, distributions from a qualified retirement plan will be subject to ordinary tax rates.

The key detriment of electing to treat distributions of employer stock as a lump-sum is that the employee's basis in the stock is subject to ordinary income treatment. A detriment, for estate tax purposes, is that NUA is considered income in respect of a decedent.

TAX PLANNING: Taxpayers may roll over part of their employee stock into an IRA and use the net unrealized appreciation treatment for the balance. Taxpayers, therefore, may optimize their savings by transferring high-basis stock to an IRA while using low-basis stock for the net unrealized appreciation treatment.[19]

¶912 Early Collection of Social Security Benefits Can Have Significant Long-Term Consequences

The time at which an individual begins collection of social security benefits can have significant long-term consequences, both in terms of absolute dollars received and in terms of exposure to market risk. Early collection of Social

---

[18] Code Sec. 402(e)(4).

[19] More detailed information on the operation of and planning for distributions of appreciated employer stock is contained in "Revisiting Net Unrealized Appreciation: A Tax-Wise Strategy that may Realize More Benefits than Ever," by John A. Nersesian and Frances L. Potter, *Journal of Financial Planning*, February 2004, Vol. 17 (2), p. 50.

Security benefits can significantly reduce the ability of an individual to withstand high and/or sustained levels of inflation. A consequence of such action is that an investor may need to adjust his portfolio to compensate for this lack of protection. A basic protective action, for example, might be to reduce one's holdings of stocks, since such investments have often fared relatively poorly during times of high inflation. A significant detriment of such action, however, is that in addition to losing opportunities to benefit from capital appreciation, the investor also loses the ability to benefit from favorable capital gains tax rates.

Example 13: Donna and Diane Edwards, twins, are both age 66 in 2008. Donna begins collecting $20,000/year in Social Security benefits during that year. Diane delays collection of benefits for four years.

Listed below is the amount of the benefits each would be collecting for three different levels of inflation for three different ages.

Age	2% Infl.		4% Infl.		6% Infl.	
	Donna	Diane	Donna	Diane	Donna	Diane
76	$24,400	$33,100	$29,600	$39,900	$35,800	$48,000
86	$29,800	$40,400	$43,800	$59,100	$64,100	$85,900
96	$36,300	$49,300	$64,800	$87,400	$114,700	$145,200

If inflation turned out to be high, 6 percent, Diane, at age 86, would be drawing over $20,000/year more than Donna. This extra income might be particularly helpful were stocks to be performing poorly, as has often been the case during periods of high inflation.

.01 Early Collection of Social Security Benefits—A Potentially Costly and Risky Choice

Individuals who begin collecting Social Security payments prior to full retirement age can potentially lose a variety of benefits, including the following:

- Loss of significant increases in inflation-adjusted benefits,
- Loss of opportunities to increase level of income subject to a minimum 15 percent federal exclusion,
- Loss of opportunities to increase level of income subject to state and local income tax exclusion, and
- Loss of a disproportionate level of spousal benefits.

Example 14: John Grey retires in 2022 at age 62 and begins drawing Social Security benefits. The age required for receiving full retirement benefits in 2022 is 67. For purposes of this example it is assumed that the maximum full benefit [retirement at normal retirement date] would be $40,000.[20] Since John is retiring five years ahead of the full retirement date, his benefits are reduced by approximately 30 percent to $28,000/year. The inflation rate, for purposes of the cost of living adjustment is assumed to be

---

[20] As a point of comparison, the maximum level of full Social Security retirement benefits in 2002 is $19,920.

4 percent per year. At age 82, John's annual benefit would be approximately $61,300.

Alternatively, if John had chosen to delay his retirement until the normal retirement date he would receive, at age 82, an annual benefit of $87,600, or more than $25,000 what he receives based on receiving early retirement benefits. Further, at least 15 percent and possibly more of this income is excluded from federal tax and, normally, this income will not be subject to state and local taxes. Importantly, his higher level of income at age 82 provides him with a valuable higher base for the collection of future Social Security benefits. If, assuming a four percent rate of inflation, he were to still be receiving benefits at age 92, his annual benefit would be approximately $130,000. Alternatively, the benefit based on initial collection at age 62 would be approximately $91,000.

Some investors prefer to begin the collection of Social Security benefits early because they want to be assured that in the event they die early, that they and/or their beneficiaries will receive a significant level of benefits. These investors can, with the extra inflow of funds, directly invest them with the objective of compensating for the loss of any future inflation-adjusted benefits. Two factors, however, can make it challenging to meet this objective:

1. Earnings from the reinvested funds are subject to taxation, and

2. Investments in stocks or other items subject to preferred capital gains rates may not provide adequate inflation protection.

Stocks, as stated previously, often perform poorly when inflation is high.

TAX PLANNING: Investors who prefer to begin collecting retirement benefits early but, nonetheless, desire inflation-protection "just in case" they outlive their actuarially projected life expectancy, may find Treasury-Inflation Protection Securities and/or I-bonds to be beneficial in terms of providing inflation protection.

PRACTICE POINTER: Presentations to clients of examples, such as the one above, may be eye-openers in terms of illustrating the effects of inflation and the magnitude of the absolute dollars that may be required to adequately fund one's retirement.

.02 Early Collection of Social Security Benefits Can Disproportionately Reduce Spouse's Benefits

Married individuals, at age 65, are generally entitled, at a minimum, to receive benefits equal to 50 percent of their spouse's primary insurance amount (PIA), the benefit paid at normal retirement age. If, however, the individual were to receive a greater benefit based on his own contributions, that amount would be used instead.

In cases where an individual's benefits are based on those received by his or her spouse, the level of benefits received will be reduced where the spouse had elected to begin early collection of social security benefits. Further, if both parties collect early, there can be a disproportionately large reduction in the amount of the benefits received.

> **Example 15:** Jerry Mullins retired in 1999 at age 62. Full benefits for an individual who retired at age 65 are assumed to have been $12,000. Since Jerry began collecting benefits three years early, his benefits are reduced by approximately 20 percent to $9,600. His wife, Joni, begins collecting benefits in 2002, at which point she is age 65. If her benefits are based on her spouse's she will receive benefits equal to 50 percent of $9,600 or $4,800. As a result of Jerry's early collection of Social Security benefits, not only are his benefits reduced but Joni's are reduced as well.

> **Example 16:** Same facts as in Example 15, except that Joni also retired in 1999, at which point she was age 62. Instead of receiving benefits based on 50 percent of $9,600, she will receive benefits based on 37.5 percent of that amount, or $3,600.

> **Example 17:** Both spouses retire at full retirement age. Jerry receives benefits of $12,000/year and Joni receives benefits of $6,000/year for a total of $18,000/year. *Example does not take into account inflation adjustments.*

In all cases the amounts shown would be adjusted for inflation. As explained in the previous section, not only does early retirement result in a reduction in current benefits, but it also results in reductions of income that is excluded for federal and state and local income tax purposes. Each year, as benefit payments are increased for inflation there is a further loss of potential tax exclusion benefits.

.03 Delayed Collection of Social Security Benefits Can Bring Disproportionate Increase in Survivor Benefits

While early collection of Social Security benefits can potentially result in a disproportionate loss of spousal benefits, delayed collection can potentially result in a disproportionate increase in Social Security benefits. Delayed collection can potentially be highly advantageous where there is a significant age difference between the primary Social Security recipient and his or her spouse. A tax advantage of this deferral is that no income is recognized until the Social Security benefits are actually collected.

A surviving spouse, age 65 or older, is generally entitled to a benefit equal to 100 percent of what his spouse was receiving in the year of death. The basis of this benefit includes any adjustment for early or delayed retirement. The annual increase in payments for delayed retirement will be 6 percent per year for those born in 1935 or 1936, 6.5 percent for those born in 1937 or 1938, 7 percent for those born in 1939 or 1940, 7.5 percent for those born in 1941 or 1942, and 8 percent for those born in 1943 or a later year, possibly making delayed collection a more attractive option for many investors. These increases are added to the annual inflation adjustments. No increase in benefits, however, is provided for delaying the collection of social security benefits past age 70.

Example 18: Mark Brocks is age 66 in 2009 at which point he is eligible to receive full Social Security benefits, assumed to be $20,000/year. Mark's wife, Maria, age 56, will ultimately receive benefits based on Mark's Social Security coverage.

Inflation is assumed to be increasing at 4 percent/year

Mark delays collecting Social Security benefits for four years in order to take advantage of the 8 percent annual benefits increase [plus inflation]. As a result, Mark begins collecting benefits in 2013 at a rate of approximately $31,500/year.

In 2019, Mark dies, at which point Maria, now age 66 begins receiving $40,000/year in benefits, equal to 100 percent of what Mark was drawing in his final year of life.

In 2049, Maria dies at age 96. In her final year of life her annual benefits are $129,600, 35 percent higher than what she would have received, $96,000, had Mark not delayed collection of Social Security benefits.

PRACTICE POINTER: The survivor benefits available for married couples with a significantly younger spouse are unlikely to be available through a commercial annuity or any other source. Whereas a commercial annuity company would normally take into account the combined life expectancy of two spouses, resulting in a reduction of payments, Social Security, as a matter of public policy, provides a guaranteed 100 percent survivor's benefit, regardless of a couple's combined life expectancy.

.04 Women May Receive Greater Benefits from Deferring Social Security Benefits

While adjustments for early or delayed payments of Social Security benefits are gender neutral, the reality is that women, on average, live longer than men. Factors such as current health and genetics affect longevity, of course, but, in general, women are more likely than men to benefit from electing to delay benefits. The following categories of women, based only on life expectancies, may benefit more from delaying benefits than men:

1. Unmarried women,

2. Married women whose benefits would not be determined by reference to their husband's earnings, and

3. Married women whose husband's benefits would not be determined by reference to their own.

Alternatively, married individuals, both men and women, whose benefits are determined by reference to another may not find delaying collection of their own benefits to be advantageous because it may not result in any increase in total benefits.

¶912.04

¶913 Proper Choices for Investment Type and Income Timing May Reduce Taxability of Social Security Benefits

Taxpayers who have *provisional income* over $25,000 may be required to include a portion of their Social Security benefits as taxable income.[21] Provisional income, in general, is comprised of one half of Social Security benefits, adjusted gross income, tax-exempt interest, and certain tax-preferred benefits such as adoption assistance, foreign earned income, and savings bonds proceeds used for education purposes.[22] If provisional income is under $25,000 for single taxpayers or under $32,000 for married taxpayers, filing jointly, none of the Social Security benefits are subject to tax. Taxpayers who have provisional income over that amount may be required to include as much as 85 percent of those benefits in income.

While the threshold levels may initially seem too low to avoid inclusion of benefits, careful choice of investment assets and timing of income recognition may make it possible for even taxpayers of relatively significant means to avoid inclusion of benefits. Opportunities for avoidance of inclusion may be greater where the taxpayer has funds in a Roth IRA and is not required to take taxable distributions from a retirement account.

Example 19: Bob and Bernice Laing, a married couple filing jointly, both age 66 are retired and together draw $30,000/year in Social Security benefits. Their assets are as follows:

Traditional IRAs (rolled over from qualified plans)	$1,500,000
Roth IRAs	150,000
I–bonds (not currently taxable)	250,000
Corporate bond fund (6% annual income)	200,000
Individual utility stocks (4% annual income)	100,000
Money market fund (2% annual income)	50,000
Total assets	$2,250,000

Bob and Bernice fund their current lifestyle by drawing upon their Social Security benefits and income generated by the corporate bond fund, the individual utility stocks and the money market fund. Also, where additional funds are required they take nontaxable distributions from their Roth IRAs. Their total provisional income is as follows:

1/2 Social Security benefits	$15,000
Corporate bond interest	12,000
Utility stock dividends	4,000
Money market interest	1,000
Total provisional income	$32,000

---

[21] A detailed discussion of computations and method for planning to reduce the inclusion of Social Security benefits is contained in "Minimizing the Taxability of Social Security Benefits," by Seth Hammer, *The Tax Adviser*, September 1997, pp. 566-574.

[22] "Provisional income" is not defined in the Code or regulations, but is referred to in H. Rep. No 103-111, 103d Cong., 1st Sess.654 (1993) 1999-3 CB 230.

Social Security benefits are not required to be included in taxable income because taxable income is not more than $32,000.

Note that the actual cash generated here is $47,000, not $32,000, since only half of the Social Security benefits are included for purposes of the provisional income computation. If Bob and Bernice do require additional cash they could potentially draw $50,000/year from their Roth IRA for three years, allowing them to generate almost $100,000 cash/year, without having any of their Social Security benefits subject to income tax.

TAX PLANNING: Other investments that may be effective for minimizing provisional income include exchange-traded shares and S&P 500 index shares. Purchases of annuities may also be particularly helpful in allowing a taxpayer to draw cash and defer recognition of interest income until later years.

Example 20: Lucy Smith, age 66, invests $300,000 in a commercial (nonqualified) annuity paying a fixed 6 percent return per year. Although annual payments are approximately $26,155/year, the amount she will be required to currently include in income is only $11,155. This amount of required income recognition represents deferred interest of $6,845 in the first year. Lucy's other investments are an IRA (traditional) valued at $1,000,000 and $200,000 in short-term bonds yielding 4 percent/year. Lucy also receives $12,000 in Social Security benefits per year.

1/2 Social Security benefits	$6,000
Annuity income	11,155
Bond interest income	8,000
Total provisional income	$25,155

Although the total cash generated for the year was $46,155 [annuity $26,100 + Social Security $12,000 + bond interest income $8,000], Lucy is required to include only $78 in Social Security benefits in income (lesser of one half of provisional income in excess of $25,000 or one half of Social Security benefits).

If this cash generated was insufficient, Lucy would have several reasonable options to increase it, at no or minimal tax cost.

1. **Liquidate bonds.** Lucy could liquidate bonds in the amount of $40,000/year for five years without increasing income. Actual bond interest income would fall from the decline in principal. Lucy could simply shift assets within her IRA in order to maintain her desired level of asset allocation.

2. **Convert bonds to annuities.** Lucy could liquidate the bonds and increase her annuity investment by $200,000. This would generate net cash of $9,437 ($17,437 additional annuity payments—8,000 lost interest income). Although cash would increase, provisional income would actually decrease slightly: $7,437 taxable annuity income -

$8,000 in foregone bond interest=$533 net decrease in provisional income.

3. **Draw limited funds from IRA.** Lucy could draw funds up to the provisional income level of $34,000 and be subject only to a maximum inclusion rate of 50 percent. The higher inclusion rate, 85 percent, applies for single individuals to income levels above $34,000.

Example 21: Same as the previous example except taxable annuity income is $11,000 and Lucy withdraws $9,000 from her IRA. As a result, Lucy's provisional income is $34,000 and, therefore, she is required to include $4,500 of Social Security benefits in income.

Note that the distribution of $9,000 from the IRA results in a total inclusion of $13,500 in income, after taking into account the $4,500 of taxable Social Security benefits. The distribution from the IRA, therefore results in a multiplier effect of 50 percent. Since Lucy, without the multiplier effect, is only subject to a 15 percent tax bracket, the effect of the multiplier effect is modest, increasing the effective tax rate for drawing from the IRA to 22.5 percent (1.5 x 15%).

The multiplier effect can, however, have a more dramatic effect where the taxpayer is in a higher tax bracket and subject to an 85 percent phase-in rate for inclusion of Social Security benefits. If for example, Lucy was in a 25 percent tax bracket and her Social Security benefits were subject to the 85 percent phase-in rate, the economic tax rate for that distribution would be 46.25 percent (25% x 1.85).

Chapter 10

GIFTS AND ESTATES

¶1001 EGTRRA Creates Uncertainty, but also Opportunities

The uncertainty surrounding the future of estate and gift taxes following passage of the Economic Growth and Tax Relief Reconciliation Act of 2001 (EGTRRA) creates a variety of challenges for estate planners. EGTRRA provides for a gradual reduction in the amount of dollars subject to estate tax, leading to a full suspension in 2010, but provides for a full reinstatement in the year 2011. The gift tax is not repealed, but the total amount of the gift tax exclusion is increased permanently to at least 1 million dollars. Carryover basis of assets for decedents dying after 2009 is limited to 1.3 million dollars plus an additional $3 million is allowed for spouses. The primary reason for this peculiar pattern of suspension followed by reinstatement is the "Byrd Rule," Section 313 of the Congressional Budget Act of 1974, that provides that tax cuts cannot be made permanent unless they are paid for by permanent spending cuts or unless 60 senators vote to waive the rule.

Planners, subject to this quandary, could potentially establish plans in accordance with assumptions of either:

1. The temporary estate tax repeal will be made permanent, or

2. The estate tax will be reinstated in 2011.

A third course of action, however, may make the most sense:

- Take advantage of benefits allowed during the period through 2010 (e.g., increase amount of gifts),

- Develop flexible planning strategies that can be adapted to future law changes, and

- Develop hedging strategies, such as the purchase of universal life insurance, to litigate the future changes.

.01 JGTRRA Creates Additional Uncertainty and Opportunities

The Jobs and Growth Tax Relief Reconciliation Act of 2003 creates more uncertainty and opportunities in the area of gifts and estates by lowering tax rates for dividends and capital gains, but making the provisions subject to sunset provisions. Further complicating planning efforts is that the sunset provisions for the lowered dividends and capital gains tax rates take effect in 2009, whereas the sunset provisions for gift, estate, and generation skipping transfers take effect in 2011.

¶1002 EGTRRA Provides Expanded Opportunities to Reduce Assets, Potentially Subject to Estate Tax, through Gift Transactions

Taxpayers whose level of assets could potentially make their estates subject to estate tax, either in its present or some revised form, may wish to avail themselves of opportunities to reduce their potential estates through gift transactions. EGTRRA provides for a permanent increase in the aggregate gift exemption to $1,000,000. Taxpayers, therefore, who gave out the full $675,000, allowable under prior law, may wish to make an additional $325,000 in gifts in order to immediately reduce their current estate and reduce the probability of future appreciation remaining within the estate. The transfer of property also reduces the amount of property potentially subject to built-in capital gains within the estate, effective 2010.

Taxpayers who have already given out more than $675,000 and paid gift taxes for gifts made prior to 2002, may not be able to take full advantage of the $325,000 increase in the exemption because of the marginal increase in gift tax rates.

> **Example 1:** Alice has made taxable gifts of $1,500,000 through 2001. As a result she has paid gift taxes of $335,250 [$555,800 tax – credit of $220,550]. She made no taxable gifts in 2002 or 2003. In 2004 she makes a gift of $325,000. She will be required to pay a gift tax of $21,000 [$702,050 tax - $345,800 credit - $335,250 previous taxes paid]. In this situation the maximum amount she could give without incurring further gift tax liability would be $278,333 [$278,333 x .45 marginal tax rate=$125,250 (increase in credit amount from 2001 to 2002).

A second consideration, where gifts have been made beyond the exemption amount, is whether to make such gifts now or wait until the gift tax rate is lowered to 35 percent in 2010. The gift tax rate is scheduled for reinstatement at a maximum rate of 55 percent in 2011.

> **PRACTICE POINTER:** The key factors in determining whether a taxpayer who has already used the full allowable gift exemption should make gifts currently or wait until 2010 depends upon:
>
> 1. Current marginal gift tax rate,
> 2. Future marginal gift tax rate,
> 3. Assumed after-tax rates of return for the assets to be gifted, and
> 4. Assumed after-tax rates of return for funds that would otherwise be used to pay current gift taxes.

¶1003 $55,000 Gifts to Section 529 Qualified Tuition Programs May Provide Up-Front Gift Tax Benefit and Unusual Revocability Feature

Taxpayers can make gifts of up to $55,000 to a Section 529 qualified tuition program and elect to have it treated as if it had been made over a period of five years.[1] Therefore, a taxpayer making such a gift will not have to use up any of his unified credit. Added benefits of making such a gift is that the donor can change designated family members as beneficiaries and, importantly, could ultimately be used by the donor, subject to taxable income and a ten percent penalty.

> **Example 2:** Jim and Joan, age 70 each make $55,000 gifts, for a total of $110,000 to a qualified tuition program to benefit their granddaughter, Jeanette, age 1 and/or future grandchildren. Although Jim and Joan's intent is that the funds be used for their grandchildren's benefit they would prefer, nonetheless, to have access to the funds "just in case" they need them.

> Twenty years later, Jim and Joan are both alive at age 90 and, due to inflation, need to use half of the funds, now valued at $500,000 for current living expenses. The amount they withdraw for their own use would be subject to income taxes and an additional excise tax. Despite these requirements, Jim and Joan reason that this detriment may be relatively minor since they have benefited from twenty years of tax-deferred growth. Also, the half that is used for the grandchildren's benefit is totally excluded from tax.

¶1004 Unlimited Gifts of Tuition Payments and Medical Expenses Can Be Made without Affecting Annual Exclusion

A donor is entitled to an unlimited gift tax exclusion for payments made directly to an educational organization for tuition and for payments made directly to heath care providers for medical services.

In the case of education expenses, only direct payments for tuition qualify for the unlimited exclusion. Payments for other expenses, such as room and board, are subject to the $11,000 annual exclusions.

Beneficiaries of tuition and/or medical payments are not required to be dependents of the taxpayers. Further, payments of medical expenses are not subject to any percentage limitations.

¶1005 Gifts of Appreciated Property to Students and/or Low Income Taxpayers Can Provide Income and Transfer Tax Benefits

Gifts of appreciated stock, in addition to reducing an individual's potential taxable estate can also provide income tax benefits, including lower marginal rates for ordinary income, capital gains and dividends.

> **Example 3:** Sam and Susan Sanders, taxpayers subject to a marginal ordinary tax rate of 35 percent, make gifts of the following assets to their daughters, Emily, Johanna, and Wendy, respectively. All of the daughters are students subject to marginal ordinary tax rates of 15 percent.

---

[1] Code Sec. 529(c)(2)(b) provides for the five-year allowance. Rev. Proc. 2001-59 (2001-52 IRB) an-nounced an increase in the annual gift tax exclusion from $10,000 to $11,000.

Gift to Emily:	Stock with a fair market value of $22,000 and a basis of $20,000. The stock pays dividends of $220/year. The dividends qualify for reduced tax rates.
Gift to Johanna:	Shares in a real estate investment trust (REIT) with a fair market value of $22,000 and a basis of $20,000. The REIT pays dividends of $660/year. The dividends do not qualify for reduced tax rates.
Gift to Wendy:	Ginnie Mae unit with a fair market value of $22,000, a basis of $22,000, and a face value of $25,000. The Ginnie Mae investment is expected to generate interest income of $660/year.

Each daughter sold or redeemed her investment after three years for $25,000. As a result of these transfers, Sam and Susan Sanders achieved the following income tax benefits:[2]

Gift to Emily:	Capital Gain: $5,000 x 10%	$500
	Dividends: $220 x 3 x 10%	66
		$566
Gift to Johanna	Capital Gain: $5,000 x 10%	$500
	Nonqualifying dividends: $660 x 3 x 20%	396
		$896
Gift to Wendy	Ordinary Income: $3,000 x 20%	$600
	Interest payments: $660 x 3 x 20%	396
		$996

As a result of this transfer, the parents' receive the greatest income tax benefit from transferring the Ginnie Mae investment, even though there is greater capital appreciation in the stock and REIT investments.

¶1006 Careful Choice of Assets Can Mitigate Effect of Complex Trust's High Marginal Tax Rates

Investors, for a variety of reasons, may prefer to place assets in a complex trust for an extended period of time. Parents, for example, may wish, in the event of their death, to have life insurance proceeds placed into a trust that will extend until the child reaches age 30 or even later. The reduction in tax rates, enacted by JGTRRA, potentially expands the range of feasible investments by allowing trusts the reduced rates for dividends and capital gains. Inclusion of assets within the trust that do not qualify for the reduced dividends and capital gains tax rates or are not tax-exempt, can potentially have very onerous effects. In 2004, for example, the top marginal tax rate on ordinary income for trusts, 35 percent, applies to taxable income over $9,550 (projected).

The following assets may provide good opportunities to mitigate the potentially onerous tax rates applicable for income taxable to a nongrantor trust.

---

[2] Capital gains and qualifying dividends tax benefit, 10 percent, is the difference between the parents' rate of 15 percent and the child's rate of 5 percent. Ordinary income tax benefit, 20 percent, is the difference between the parents' marginal tax bracket of 35 percent and the child's marginal tax of 15 percent.

Municipal bonds. While these investments are often thought of as conservative investments, broader based municipal bond funds can potentially provide after-tax returns that are reasonably competitive with stock funds, but with less volatility. The Russell 2000 Index, an index of small capitalization stocks, for example, generated an average annual return of 10.01 percent for the ten-year period ended September 30, 2001.[3] If an individual were subject to a 33 percent marginal tax rate, the after-tax return would be 6.71 percent. The Lehman Municipal Bond Index, alternatively, for that same time period, generated an average ten-year return of 7.05 percent, with less volatility.[4] Taxpayers considering funding a trust with municipal bond funds should, however, evaluate whether holdings of private activity bonds could result in the trust being subject to the alternative minimum tax.

Exchange-traded funds. These funds typically engage in no short-term trading that would be subject to tax at ordinary income rates. Investors considering such investments for the long-term or for contingencies, such as the funding of a life insurance trust, may wish to limit their choices for exchange-traded shares to those that are well established and are likely to have long-term viability, such as Standards and Poor's Depository Receipts (SPDRs), based on the performance of the S&P 500. A somewhat less tax-efficient alternative to exchange-traded funds would be index funds.

Common and qualifying preferred stock. While most common stocks qualify for reduced tax rates, some investments described as "preferred stock," may actually be treated as bonds and, therefore, not be eligible for benefits.

PRACTICE POINTER: As more companies increase their dividend payouts, following JGTRRA, trustees may find it cost effective to utilize dividend reinvestment plans. Such plans may reduce the transaction and management costs typically associated with a trust administered stock portfolio. Dividend reinvestment plans may also minimize or eliminate the time period where dividend payouts are held in fully taxable accounts (e.g., money markets) while awaiting reinvestment.

TAX PLANNING: Although, under current law, there is no distinction in tax rates between dividends and capital gains, advisers should be cognizant of the sunset provisions of JGTRRA that may affect long-term planning for trusts.[5] Perhaps most important is that the reduced rates for dividends are not scheduled to apply for payments for tax years beginning after December 31, 2008. Taxpayers, therefore, may find it beneficial to fund trusts with growth stocks, rather than value stocks, because the expected lower level of dividends should reduce the amount of income that is potentially subject to tax as ordinary income, following any expiration of benefits. Clients should also be advised of the uncertainties of future tax rates, arising from unforeseen political and economic conditions.

---

[3] Derived from data provided by *Morningstar Inc.*, reported at vanguard.com.

[4] *Ibid.*

[5] Act Section 303 of the Jobs and Growth Tax Relief Reconciliation Act of 2003.

¶1006

¶1007 Universal Life Insurance May Serve as a Hedge Against Uncertain Future of Estate Tax

Investors who wish to hedge the issue of whether or not they will be subject to a reinstated estate tax, following its scheduled suspension in 2010, may find it beneficial to consider the purchase of universal life insurance products designed to address this uncertainty.

Issuers of life insurance polices have addressed this uncertainty in a variety of ways including the following two methods:

Attach rider to standard universal life policy. One company's policy, for example, offers an Estate Tax Repeal Rider that allows taxpayers to cancel their policy, without surrender charges, should the estate tax repeal be extended through at least January 2, 2013.

Provide guarantee that cash value will be equal to the premium paid. This type of provision typically also provides that the insured can cancel the policy if no longer needed, as in the ease of permanent estate tax repeal, or, if needed, continue to provide coverage.

> **PRACTICE POINTER:** Purchasers of policies seeking a hedge for repeal/continuation of the estate tax should carefully review their provisions and costs. One policy, for example, provides for a waiver of surrender charges, only where there is a full surrender of the policy. Another company provides a more flexible option, in the event that the policy is no longer needed for reasons not limited to the repeal of the estate tax. Clients should be aware, however, that greater flexibility often comes with higher costs.

In cases where the estate tax, if applicable, is expected to arise only in significant amount on the death of the second spouse, consideration of second-to-die insurance may be warranted.

¶1008 2010 One-Year Suspension of the Generation-Skipping Transfer Tax Creates a Window of Opportunity

Wealthier individuals who desire to make generation-skipping transfers may mark their calendars for the year 2010, the year in which both the GST is scheduled for suspension and which the gift tax is to be reduced to a maximum rate of 35 percent. The saving in taxes can be significant, particularly in cases where the donor would otherwise be subject to the maximum GST rate.

> **Example 4:** Denise makes a generation-skipping transfer of $1,000,000 to her grandson Mike in the year 2004. The transfer is subject to both the highest GST and gift tax rates applicable in that year, 48 percent. As a result of the transfer she would be required to pay
>
> 1. GST tax of $480,000 [$1,000,000 x 48%]
> 2. Gift tax of $710,400 [($1,000,000 gift + $480,000 tax) x 48% gift tax rate]
>
> Total taxes would be $1,210,400 well over 100 percent of the amount transferred.

Example 5: Denise makes a generation-skipping transfer of $1,000,000 to her granddaughter Michelle in the year 2010. The GST tax is suspended in that year. The maximum gift tax rate is 35 percent. As a result of this transfer, Denise would be required to pay $350,000 in gift taxes and no generation-skipping taxes. Taxes for this transfer are $840,400 less than for the transfer in Example 4.

Opportunities may be also available to take advantage of the suspension of the GST though a two step process, whereby first the donor contributes the property currently, either through an irrevocable inter vivos transfer or a testamentary document and second, the transfer is made through the trust in 2010 when the GST is suspended.[6]

Taxpayers should be aware, however, that the law could well change prior to 2010.

¶1009 Minimum Distribution Regulations Provide Post-Mortem Opportunities to Use Disclaimers to Stretch Distributions of Retirement Payments

Regulations issued by the Internal Revenue Service provide significant post-mortem opportunities to stretch payments of retirement distributions.[7] Under these guidelines, taxpayers can maximize long-term deferrals of income by naming final beneficiaries as late as September 30 of the year following the year of the decedent's death.[8]

Example 6: Solomon dies at age 70, at which point he has an IRA valued at $1 million. He named his wife, Sarah, age 65, as primary beneficiary, daughter Rachel, age 40, as secondary beneficiary, and grandson Max, age 10, as third beneficiary.

Sarah, having substantial final assets of her own, elects to keep $100,000 in IRA benefits and disclaims $900,000. Rachel elects to keep $700,000 of the IRA and disclaims $200,000 to her son Max. As a result of these disclaimers, Sarah is able to exclude $900,000 plus future growth from her estate. Similarly, Rachel is able to exclude $200,000 plus future growth from her estate. Importantly, Solomon's naming of specific primary and secondary beneficiaries, provided Sarah with the flexibility, through the use of a disclaimer, to take as little or as much of the IRA account as she deemed necessary.

PRACTICE POINTER: In order for the post-mortem planning to be effective two requirements must be met:

---

[6] "Structure Generation-Skipping Gifts for Tax Savings," by Martin A. Goldberg, *Practical Tax Strategies*, October 2001, p. 196 explores in more detail the issue of how indirect transfers can be structured to minimize the tax on generation-skipping transfers.

[7] The primary applicable regulation is Reg. § 1.401(a)(9)-5. A good source for a full discussion of the minimum distribution rules is "Understanding the New Minimum Distribution Rules: January 2001 Amendments to the Proposed Regs.," by Natalie B. Choate at *www.ataxplan.com*.

[8] The proposed regulations had provided an even longer deferral, December 31 of the year after the year of death.

1. The decedent must have named the primary, second and, if applicable, additional tiers of beneficiaries.

2. Disclaimers must be provided by the designated beneficiaries.

An executor does not have the power to arbitrarily name beneficiaries nor disclaim on behalf of a beneficiary.

PRACTICE POINTER: An individual who is intending to make a qualified disclaimer should make sure that:

1. It is written,

2. It identifies the property disclaimed, and

3. Is signed either by himself or his legal representative.[9]

In *Estate of Chamberlain*,[10] the Ninth Circuit upheld a Tax Court ruling that a handwritten, unsigned schedule of assets and probate inventory did not constitute a qualified disclaimer. The Ninth Circuit also affirmed the Tax Court in rejecting the taxpayer's argument that Mr. Chamberlain's intent to disclaim was clear and that was substantial compliance.

.01 2002 Final Regulations Provide Opportunities to Extend Period for Taking Required Minimum Retirement Distributions

The 2002 regulations provide a variety of opportunities to extend the payment period for distributions from qualified plans. These opportunities to extend the payout of retirement plan benefits may enhance the desirability of maximizing contributions to retirement plans as part of an individual's estate plan.

Some of the key benefits of the proposed regulations are as follows.

1. **During a taxpayer's life, required minimum distributions, with one exception, are computed for a period based on the joint life expectancy of the taxpayer and a beneficiary ten years younger, regardless of the designated beneficiary's actual age.** Under the old rules, minimum distributions, in general, were required to be made over actual joint life expectancies. Under the old rules, therefore, a 70 year-old individual with a 70 year-old spouse would be required to take distributions over a period of 20.6 years. The new rules, instead, provide for a joint life expectancy of a 70 year-old with a sixty-year old beneficiary, expanding the minimum distribution period to 27.4 years.[11] The one exception to the use of this joint life expectancy rule provides for the use of a table with even more generous terms where the spouse is more than ten years younger than the taxpayer.

2. **Life expectancies of spousal beneficiaries who are sole beneficiaries are recomputed annually.** No election is required for this treatment, as was required prior to the proposed regulations. An additional benefit, in

---

[9] 26 C.F.R. 25.2518-2(b)(1).

[10] *T.J. Chamberlain Est.*, CA-9, 2001-1 USTC ¶60,407. Aff'ing (unpublished opinion), 77 TCM 2080, Dec. 53,402(M), TC Memo. 1999-181.

[11] The final regulations provide a distribution that is even more generous than under the proposed regulations. In this example, under the proposed regulations, the required minimum distribution period was 26.2 years.

¶1009.01

some cases, is that the spouse may be able to defer distributions until the year that the donor would have reached age 70 1/2.

3. **Required minimum distributions to nonspousal beneficiaries, following the death of the owner, are made over the actual life expectancy of the beneficiary.** This amount is reduced by one year for each year following the year of initial distribution. This opportunity for deferral for exclusion can be particularly great where the beneficiary is young.

Example 7: Nadiya, age ten, is the beneficiary of decedent's IRA. At age ten, her life expectancy is 72.8 years, resulting in a required distribution in the amount of 1.37 percent of total assets.[12] At age 11, her life expectancy, is reduced by one year to 71.8 years, and she is subject to a required distribution in the amount of 1.39 percent.

¶1010 Post-Mortem Elections for Savings Bonds Can Minimize Income Taxes

An executor of an estate owning U.S. Savings Bonds has the option of either electing to include the income in either the decedent's final tax return or in the estate's tax return. In many cases inclusion in the decedent's final tax return will be beneficial because:

1. The marginal income tax rate for the estate is high, as is often the case with their very compressed rate schedule, and/or

2. The marginal tax rate for the decedent is low, as might be the case where the taxpayer died early in the year.

Alternatively, in an unusual situation, where, for example, the interest is the only item subject to tax, it may be beneficial to take advantage of the estate's limited 15 percent tax bracket and $600 exemption.

If an estate elects to recognize income, it can reelect to defer recognition of income accrued after death until the bonds are redeemed. Further, the estate's election is not binding on its beneficiaries. In cases where savings bonds are reissued in a beneficiary's name, he or she can defer recognition of income until the bonds are redeemed.[13]

¶1011 Broad Interpretation of "Personal Residence" Provides Expanded Opportunities for Use of Qualified Personal Residence Trusts (QPRT)

Qualified personal residence trusts (QPRTs) provide opportunities for individuals to potentially remove significant portions of the value of their residences, including "appurtenant structures" and "adjacent land" from their taxable estate. Broad interpretations by the Service of the meanings of "appurtenant structures" and "adjacent land," may provide expanded opportunities to use this estate planning vehicle. The uncertain future of the estate tax, however, may make this a less desirable transaction for a number of taxpayers (see ¶1012).

---

[12] Life expectancy per Reg. §1.401(a)(9)-9 – Life Expectancy and distribution period tables.

[13] Rev. Rul. 58-435, 1958-2 CB 370 and Rev. Proc. 99-49, 1999-2 CB 725.

QPRTs operate through a transfer by the owner of a qualifying residence to a trust established to benefit the donees. The donor, however, rather than relinquishing all rights to the property, retains the use of it for a designated number of years. Since the donee does not have ownership of the property until the trust expires, the value of the property, for gift tax purposes, is reduced in accordance with the valuation tables prescribed in Section 7520. The longer is the term of the trust, the larger is the valuation discount. If, however, the donor dies while the terms of the trust are in effect, the full value of the property is included in her estate. Older donees, therefore, in general, will use shorter trust periods.

The Service has indicated in a series of letter rulings that it will interpret the meaning of "appurtenant structures" and "adjacent land" liberally. Some examples:

Adjacent land. In PLR 200112018, a husband and wife owned a vacation house and guest house, an 8.7 acre main lot, a one-seventh interest in an undivided interest in a 16.7 woodland preserve, and easements granting rights of access. All of the property was assessed as one unit for property tax purposes. The Service ruled that the entire property would qualify meet the qualifications for a personal residence trust under Section 2702. The fact that the woodland preserve and main lot were separate parcels, apparently did not disqualify them as adjacent properties.

Other letter rulings have approved large parcels of land as qualifying as adjacent land for purposes of qualifying for a personal residence trust: PLR 9739024 (41 acres) and 9639064 (43 acres).

Appurtenant structures. Guesthouses and ancillary apartments, even where rented have qualified for personal residence trusts: PLR 199916030 (rented), 199908032 and 9827037.

> **PRACTICE POINTER:** Although these private letter rulings lack official precedent, they do provide an indication of Service's view on these issues. Additionally, if there is a concern that a property transfer will not qualify, a taxpayer may be well advised to obtain a ruling prior to entering into the transaction.

.01 Potential Risks of QPRTs Following EGTRRA

The uncertain future of the estate tax, following EGTRRA, creates additional risks for taxpayers considering entering into a QPRT transaction.

1. If the donor uses the property as a principal residence and dies after 2009, the donee potentially would not be able to take advantage of the $250,000 exclusion available to estates for sale of a qualified personal residence. This provision, however, allowing estates to claim the exclusion becomes effective for decedents dying after December 31, 2009, but, as with many other provisions of the EGTRRA expires for decedents dying after December 31, 2010.

2. If the taxpayer dies in 2010, when there is no estate tax, or during a year where the gross estate would be less than the exemption amount, the

taxpayer would receive no estate tax benefit, while the donees would lose the opportunity to benefit from a step-up in basis.

TAX PLANNING: The benefit of QPRTs diminishes as the Section 7520 rate decreases. This result arises because the lower rate increases the value of the remainder interest that is treated as a taxable gift. As a result, in the period of 2001-2003, for example, when short-term interest rates were at historic lows, establishments of QPRTs may have been less advantageous.

Where low interest rates arise as a result of a weak economy, prospects for short-term appreciation of property may be weak. Since, however, a typical QPRT is likely to have a duration of at least five years, short-term economic considerations may be less of a consideration.

¶1012 Lower Interest Rates May Create an Enhanced Opportunity to Reduce Taxable Estates through Private Annuities

Lower interest rates allow taxpayers to transfer property in exchange for lower annuity payments, providing opportunities to minimize a taxable estate. This strategy might be used, for example, where a wealthy parent desires to transfer property to a child in exchange for the lowest allowable annuity payment.

> **Example 8:** Maria, age 75, transfers $1,000,000 in property in November 2001 to her son, Marty, in exchange for a private annuity. The Code Sec. 7520 rate for that month is 5.0 percent.[14] Marty is required to make annual payments of $129,904 [$1,000,000/7.698 annuity factor][15] in order for Maria to avoid making a gift. In contrast, the applicable rate for March 2000 was 8.2 percent. In that case, the payment required for a 75-year old individual would have been $156,993.

The annuity tables may not be used, however, in cases where an individual in failing health is considered to have at least a 50 percent probability of dying within one year.[16]

> **PRACTICE POINTER:** The total benefit of this strategy will depend upon future market interest rates. The strategy would be most effective in cases where the decline in market interest rates proved to be temporary, followed by an increase in market yields. While future interest rates cannot, of course, be predicted with a high level of accuracy, taxpayers may wish to consider this strategy during periods of lower market rates.

¶1013 Flexible Credit Shelter Trust after EGTRRA May Allow Planning without Annual Revisions

Credit shelters, also referred to as "bypass trusts," are typically designed to maximize usage of the decedent's estate tax exemption and thereby avoid

---

[14] Rev. Rul. 2001-52.

[15] Factor is per IRS Publication 1457, *Actuarial Values, Book Aleph*, Table S.

[16] Reg. § 25.7520-3(b)(3).

taxation in the decedent's estate or, later, upon the death of her spouse. Prior to the passage of EGTRRA, designations for credit shelters of either a fixed dollar amount or an amount equal to the federal estate exemption in the year of death, provided reasonably effective estate planning. Following the passage of EGTRRA, however, the scheduled increase in the amount of the allowable estate tax exemption, coupled with uncertainty whether such provisions will remain in effect, increases the importance of either including flexibility within a will's provisions or making frequent updates to the will itself.

Four methods and their related results for funding a credit shelter trust are illustrated below.

Example 9: Barney dies in 2003 with a total gross estate of $2.5 million. His will provides that proceeds from the estate are to be used first to fund a credit shelter trust equal to the maximum amount allowed in the year of death. The remainder is to be paid to his wife. Since the death occurred in 2003, the credit shelter trust receives $1 million and his wife receives $1.5 million.

Example 10: Same facts as in Example 9, except that Barney dies in the year 2006. In this case, the credit shelter trust receives $2,000,000 and his wife receives only $500,000, less than what Barney had originally intended.

Example 11: Bernadette dies in 2008 with a gross estate of $3 million. Her will specified that a credit shelter trust should be sheltered to the maximum allowable, but not to exceed 50 percent of her gross assets. As a result, the credit shelter is funded with $1.5 million, less than the $2 million dollar allowable exemption, but in accordance with her desire to provide more assets for her husband.

In some cases providing flexibility in how a trust's funds may be used may provide sufficient comfort for couples to increase the amount to be funded with a credit shelter trust.

Example 12: Marvin, age 85, has approximately $6 million in assets. Madelyn, age 75, his wife, has approximately $1 million in assets. They have minimal joint assets. Marvin's first priority, in the event he predeceases his wife, is that she can continue to live in the comfortable lifestyle to which she is accustomed. He would, however, if possible, prefer to minimize estate taxes payable upon his death.

Marvin, in 2004, prepares a will that provides for a credit shelter trust with the following provisions:

1. Fully fund the credit shelter trust to the extent of maximum allowable exemption, with the exception that spouse must receive at least $1 million,

2. Spouse is to be the trustee of the trust,

3. Spouse can take up to 5 percent of the trust annually for any reason,

4. Spouse can use principal for health, education, and support, and

5. Couple's children, upon spouse's death, will receive remaining principal.

Marvin dies in 2009 at age 92. Due to some financial setbacks and extensive medical costs the total value of his portfolio has declined to $3.75 million. Although the maximum allowable exemption for a credit shelter trust in 2009 is $3.5 million, the trust is only funded with $2.75 million, since $1 million is required by his will to be directly bequeathed to his spouse.

Madelyn will likely use trust principal first for housing and support costs (e.g., food and clothing) and then use the 5 percent allowance for luxury items such as vacations. Alternatively, if Madelyn does not require the funds, she does not have to draw upon them and she can continue to let them growth within the trust.

PRACTICE POINTER: A credit shelter trust can also provide the trustee spouse with a limited power of appointment allowing him how to decide how funds should be distributed to the couple's children. The surviving spouse could, for example, make a disproportionate distribution to a child to help with medical or educational expenses.

¶1014 QTIPs Provide Excellent Opportunities to Designate Second Tier Beneficiaries while Deferring and/or Reducing Estate Taxes

Qualified terminable interests in property can potentially provide four valuable benefits:

- Postpone estate tax until the death of the second spouse,
- Reduce total estate taxes by deferring taxation until a time when there is a higher estate tax exemption,
- Provide income for a spouse while ensuring that the underlying property is transferred to another beneficiary (e.g., child from a first marriage), and
- Provide flexibility to postpone the naming of final beneficiaries.

.01 Use with Credit Shelter Trust Can Reduce Estate Taxes

QTIPs are often used in conjunction with credit shelter trusts because exclusive use of QTIPS can potentially result in an increased estate tax liability at the death of the second spouse.

Example 13: Morris, age 75 holds assets valued at $3 million. His wife, Mona, age 73, holds assets valued at $2 million. If Morris were to die in 2004 and leave all of his assets to Mona, either through a direct bequest, qualifying for the unlimited marital deduction, and/or a QTIP trust, none of his estate would be taxable, but the full $3 million from his estate, plus any appreciation [for the direct bequest] would be taxable to her estate.

Alternatively, if Morris were to leave $1.5 million to a credit shelter trust then that amount, equal to the 2004 exclusion, would not be subject to estate tax.

.02 *Clayton QTIPs* Provide Potentially Valuable Post-Death Power of Appointment

A *Clayton QTIP*, provides the executor or the trustee with power to appoint property for which the marital deduction is not elected, to a nonmarital trust.[17] This opportunity to defer the decision on the allocation of property until after the death of the first spouse can potentially provide substantial flexibility that can be used to reduce estate tax. If, for example, after the death of a husband, his wife determined that she did not need the full amount allowable for inclusion in a QTIP, the trustee could make an election for only a partial QTIP election and subsequently increase the amount that is funded in a credit shelter trust.

A limitation of this planning technique, however, is that the power to make this decision should normally not be done by a spouse trustee since the IRS could argue that the allocation of the nonelected QTIP portion constitutes a taxable gift.[18] Some taxpayers, despite the potential tax benefits, may not be comfortable leaving such a decision in the hands of anyone other than themselves.

> **PLANNING POINTER:** The determination of whether to use a credit shelter trust and/or a QTIP depends on an individual's goals. QTIPs are commonly used in situations of second or later marriages where an individual wants to ensure that funds will be left for the benefit of her children from a previous marriage. If an individual wishes, however, to leave her spouse all of her funds, without restriction, then neither a credit shelter trust nor a QTIP should be used. Such situations may arise where the primary concern is about having enough money to maintain current lifestyles and/or there is not an "important" secondary beneficiary, as may be the case where parents are estranged from their children or there are no living children. In such cases, taxpayers may not be as concerned with the payment of estate taxes.

Passage of EGTRRA may also have created situations where taxpayers may be willing to "bet" that at the time of the second death's spouse, the amount of the estate tax exemption will either be repealed or be in excess of the allowable annual exclusion. Taxpayers may also hedge this "bet" through the purchase of universal life insurance products designed specifically to address this issue.

Wealthier individuals who are primarily concerned about leaving unrestricted money for their spouses may, nonetheless, still elect to set up at least a partial credit shelter trust in order not to waste the estate tax exemption. Again, however, if the taxpayer believes that it is likely that the estate tax exemption at the time of the spouse's death will be sufficiently large or repealed, then he may choose not to fund the trust. Similarly, the individual may also choose to hedge his decision through the purchase of an appropriate universal life insurance product.

---

[17] Usage of *Clayton* QTIPs and other estate planning techniques following passage of EGTRRA are discussed in more detail in *Estate Planning Strategies After Estate Tax Reform* by the estate planning department of Schiff, Hardin & Waite, edited by

Charles D. Fox IV and Thomas W. Abendorth, CCH, Chicago 2001.

[18] *See R.B. Regester Est.*, 83 TC 1, Dec. 41,311 (1984).

.03 QTIPs Can Provide Spouse with Limited Power of Appointment for Optimal Distribution of Assets

An individual may want to ensure that a significant portion of assets pass to designated beneficiaries, following the death of his spouse. He may not be certain, however, especially if his spouse is significantly younger, which would be the most beneficial way to distribute those assets among the beneficiaries. A child, for example, could develop health problems or a financial setback. A strategy for providing flexibility to deal with such uncertainties would be to provide the spousal beneficiary of the QTIP trust with a limited power of appointment. Under such a plan, the decedent designates who are the remainder beneficiaries, but provides the spouse with some power to determine how much each of those beneficiaries are to actually receive.

PLANNING POINTER: If the beneficiaries are children from the same marriage, the use of a limited power of appointment may be a relatively unusual occurrence. In some cases, however, such a provision might be provided where a spouse has a concern that following her death, her spouse, through remarriage or other means, may squander funds intended for use by their children.

Index

References are to paragraph (¶) numbers.

References are to paragraph (¶) numbers.

References are to paragraph (¶) numbers.

References are to paragraph (¶) numbers.

References are to paragraph (¶) numbers.

References are to paragraph (¶) numbers.

References are to paragraph (¶) numbers.

References are to paragraph (¶) numbers.

References are to paragraph (¶) numbers.

References are to paragraph (¶) numbers.

References are to paragraph (¶) numbers.

ZER